I0796075

A LOVE LETTER ...

Family Escapes

A LOVE LETTER TO THE MOST BEAUTIFUL
FAMILY-FRIENDLY HOTELS

Family Escapes

teNeues

Discover the world!

Families should fulfill their travel dreams not despite their children, but precisely *because* of them. This conviction first took shape years ago, when, as a new mother of three, I found myself sitting on a Maldivian beach in paradise. It was there that the idea for The Family Project was born: to inspire travel-loving families to embrace adventure, try new things, and discover the world with the same curiosity and wonder their children bring to it. One of my team members, a mother herself, summed it up perfectly not long ago: "With children, everything is possible—only better!"

Feeling freedom and adventure together as a family, discovering new cultures, sharing unforgettable moments, and celebrating life out in the world—to me, this is the greatest joy and the most valuable gift I can pass on to my children.

We have visited every hotel featured in this book together as a family—and for many different reasons, each has captured our hearts: magical islands, individual safari camps, authentic nature lodges, and inspiring destinations for exploration. For us, travel means slow travel—taking time for what truly matters, and for one another. We love the concept of barefoot luxury introduced by Eva and Sonu Shivdasani in the Maldives, a philosophy that has since redefined modern luxury across the globe by setting aside convention and elevating freedom to true luxury. In that same spirit, our focus has never been on classic family hotels, but on extraordinary hideaways, cozy sanctuaries that give children space to share their curiosity with us while simultaneously offering a refuge for those seeking tranquility. These are places that understand that families with children bring life and energy to a hotel. One such place is Schloss Elmau, created by Dietmar Mueller-Elmau, and one of the reasons his introductory interview on the following pages brings me such joy.

Travel is my greatest passion, and my family my most precious treasure, and with The Family Project and *Family Escapes*, both come together in the most wonderful way. Let yourself be inspired ...

Warmest,
Andrea Stadlhuber

TABLE OF CONTENTS

TIME & TIDE CHONGWE LODGE

ISLAS SECAS

East Africa

Europe

The Americas

Bucket List

Where Families Flourish and Parents Recharge

DIETMAR MUELLER-ELMAU RECREATED SCHLOSS ELMAU, A HOTEL WITH A STORIED TRADITION, AS A PLACE WHERE FAMILIES COME TOGETHER, WHILE LEAVING ENOUGH SPACE FOR EVERYONE TO ENJOY THEIR OWN FREEDOM.

Q: *Mr. Mueller-Elmau, you once said that children are what truly bring a place to life. Why was it important to you to include children in the world of Schloss Elmau?*
A: It may sound simple, but it's true. Without children, there is no future, and without children's laughter, there is no joy. I want Schloss Elmau to be a vibrant place, one that offers space for new experiences and new ideas—and that definitely includes children.

Q: *You are a father yourself, and you grew up at Schloss Elmau. How did your own childhood experiences and your experiences as a father influence your vision for reimagining Schloss Elmau?*

A: I love children as much as I love peace and quiet. Some might see that as a contradiction, but that is exactly why I wanted to bring the two together. The previous concept was "vacation from yourself," but I believe "vacation for yourself" is much more important. I rebuilt and expanded Schloss Elmau so that guests here can enjoy both vacation with and vacation from their families.

> "Without children, there is no future, and without children's laughter, there is no joy."

Q: *At peak times, Schloss Elmau hosts up to 150 children. How have you found ways to keep lively families and guests seeking tranquility equally happy?*
A: We have expansive spas, restaurants, and lounges where adult guests can enjoy freedom along with peace and quiet. At the same time, we offer the same quality of experiences to families, ensuring that all guests get what they truly want and need. We have created spaces where parents can intentionally unwind together with their children, and this parallel approach clearly works very well.

Q: *At Schloss Elmau, children don't just attend a child-care program, they also experience very special activities like chess lessons, photography workshops, and science lab courses. What defines a contemporary children's program for you?*
A: Travel is educational, so vacation hotels should offer not only relaxation, but also inspiration. That is why our

Dietmar Mueller-Elmau: "Music and literature are what give life its true meaning."

Opposite page: At Schloss Elmau, families can experience great contemporary musical artists.

edutainment workshops and soccer camps—led, by the way, by professional Bundesliga coaches—allow children to not only learn something new but also form lifelong friendships. And I am delighted that these encounters often lead to friendships among the parents as well.

Q: *Why is it important to you to introduce children to music, literature, and philosophy from an early age?*
A: Music and literature are what give life its true meaning; they expand our horizons. That is why we also have a bookstore here, for both adults and children. But the most wonderful experience is surely attending unforgettable concerts, where families can experience the great musical artists of our time together.

Q: *You have continuously evolved Schloss Elmau. What are you currently focused on, looking ahead to the future?*
A: For a year now, we have been offering AI courses in collaboration with the Technical University of Munich. In the future, I hope to offer workshops on critical and creative use of social media and debate clubs where children can hone their skepticism, judgement, and rhetorical skills.

Q: *And what inspiration do you hope families take away from their stay at Schloss Elmau?*
A: A sense of timelessness that awakens a longing to return.

Nature's Voice on Frégate Island

CONSERVATION MANAGER ANNA ZORA FOCUSES ON PRESERVING FRÉGATE ISLAND'S NATURAL WONDERS IN THE SEYCHELLES. COMBINING PASSION AND SCIENTIFIC EXPERTISE, SHE MAINTAINS THE ECOLOGICAL BALANCE AMID THE RESORT'S EXTENSIVE RENOVATIONS.

Q: *Ms. Zora, Frégate has long been regarded as a pioneer in nature conservation. The total renovation of the island resort is now almost completed. How did you ensure that such a large-scale transformation could be done in harmony with nature?*
A: Having lived and worked on Frégate Island for six years now, I immediately notice any change in the rhythm of nature. In fact, during the renovations, my team and I were able to devote even more attention to the research aspect of our work and gather valuable data on the island's ecological balance. Strict protection against invasive species remains our top priority, and because I was personally involved in the renovations from the very beginning, I was able to ensure that conservation was considered in every decision, to preserve Frégate's unique biodiversity.

Q: *The island is home to 3,500 giant tortoises and the Seychelles magpie robin, a bird once on the brink of extinction. What does it mean to you personally to live and work in such an extraordinary place, and what do you consider your greatest success?*

"Over the years, I have become familiar with the heartbeat of this ecosystem and discovered how adaptable nature is."

A: Every day my team and I remind ourselves how fortunate we are to live and work in a place of such remarkable beauty. Preserving this for future generations is, to me, our greatest achievement. Over the years, I have become familiar with the heartbeat of this ecosystem and discovered how adaptable nature is, often more than we realize.

Its uncontrollable power can only be met with respect and integrity, and when we do so, nature rewards us by flourishing.

Q: *With its organic farm and hydroponics, Frégate has taken sustainability to a new level. What makes this project unique, and could it serve as a model for other islands?*
A: Our farm of over 10 hectares is completely organic, and hydroponics is a part of that. Our goal is to meet as much of the island's needs as possible while staying true to our principles: no pesticides, no artificial fertilizers, only natural cycles. On Frégate, the soil is our "black gold," enriched daily by the native wildlife—birds, tortoises, and countless invertebrates. We also process food waste into compost, so nothing is lost in this closed cycle. With our regenerative agriculture, we want to supply the neighboring islands as well as our guests and staff. In addition to fresh produce, we also produce jams, spices, sea salt, and rum by hand here on the island. It is this combination of nature conservation, agriculture, and hospitality that makes this project so special. Everyone on the island shares responsibility for this ecosystem, allowing us to be both sustainable and productive, and to inspire other islands.

Q: *How can families actively participate in nature conservation efforts on Frégate?*
A: Nature conservation on Frégate is dynamic, interactive, and open to everyone, including the families of our guests, who can join in everywhere: planting corals, counting birds—and when children help us measure tortoises, you can see the joy and wonder in their eyes. These emotional moments leave a lasting impression, and that is what makes Frégate Island so special. We make it easy for everyone to connect deeply with nature. We will continue to offer guided hikes, talks, and nature safaris tailored to all ages. This way, every guest can be more than a spectator, and anyone who actively helps protect one of the rarest ecosystems on Earth will never forget the experience.

Q: *How do you envision the future of Frégate ten years from now? What message would you like to share with families who will visit the island?*
A: We think less in terms of ten years and more in centuries. Frégate should always be a place where tourism and nature enrich one another. Our guests should take a sense of responsibility for nature back into the world with them, showing that conservation is possible in everyday life. My message to families is: Never take nature for granted. Every day it offers us something surprising, beautiful, and fascinating. Let it inspire you to protect and preserve its wonders.

"Nature conservation on Frégate is dynamic, interactive, and open to everyone, including the families of our guests."

Above: Lined with countless coconut palm trees, Anse Victorin, on the far northwestern part of the island, was named the world's most beautiful beach by *The Times*.

Left: While snorkeling and diving in the crystal-clear waters around Frégate Island, you can enjoy incredible views of the underwater world teeming with marine life.

An Island Paradise Reinvents Itself

THE SEYCHELLES' LEGENDARY PRIVATE ISLAND WITH SEVEN PRISTINE BEACHES AND 3,500 GIANT TORTOISES HAS COMPLETED AN EXTENSIVE TRANSFORMATION—COMBINING EXCLUSIVE LUXURY WITH UNPARALLELED COMMITMENT TO CONSERVATION AND SPECIES PROTECTION NOW MORE THAN EVER.

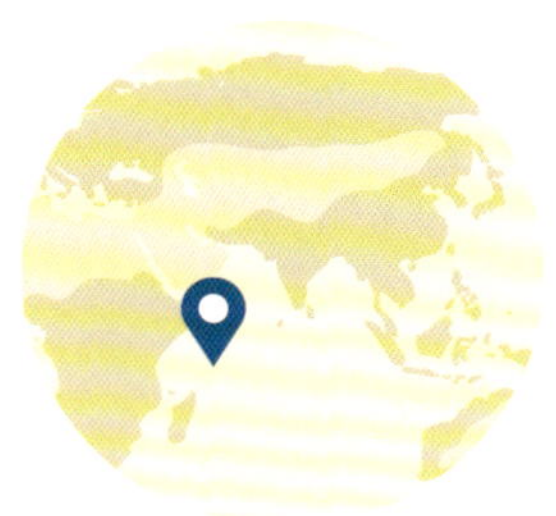

Where: Private island in the east of the Inner Seychelles, north of Madagascar in the Indian Ocean

What: 17 newly renovated villas immersed in nature with a view across the ocean
Vibe: private and exclusive, in harmony with nature and sustainable

Hidden in the enchanting turquoise expanse of the Indian Ocean, framed by granite cliffs, lush tropical greenery, and dreamlike beaches, lies Frégate Island. This private refuge is home to rare animal species and is a living showcase of conservation success. The story of the Seychelles magpie robin is particularly moving. Once reduced to a dozen surviving individuals in the world, found only on Frégate, the population has rebounded to more than 250 across the Seychelles, thanks to dedicated protection efforts.

LUXURY MEETS NATURE CONSERVATION

Frégate has reinvented itself while preserving its natural treasures—a remarkable achievement. The exclusive resort has undergone a long and extensive transformation: new roads and pathways, a revitalized spa and restaurants, and comfortable staff accommodations, the surroundings of which feel like a resort in their own right and are designed as a place to meet visitors. The new villas also combine sustainable, ecological designs with an unmatched level of luxury. With just 17 residences on the entire private island, exclusivity is assured. Each villa is an overwhelmingly spacious refuge, flooded with light and openly structured. Materials such as glass, stone, and light wood characterize the architecture, blending so naturally into nature as if it had always been there. Indoor and outdoor areas flow seamlessly together, while panoramic windows frame views of the tropical jungle and white sand beaches. Here, privacy is not merely promised; it is elevated to an art form—generous, elegant, and inseparably tied to the island itself. A unique hallmark of Frégate is its Conservation Manager and dedicated team, who not only oversaw the resort's careful redesign but also have been ensuring for years that every guest, regardless of age, has the chance to experience the broad spectrum of nature and species conservation themselves. Child-friendly nature safaris and hikes reveal the wonders in need of protection. Anyone who has had the opportunity to help plant corals or care for the impressive turtles will take this experience home with them.

HIGHLIGHTS FOR KIDS & TEENS:

- Encounters with giant tortoises, nature tours, and spontaneous animal sightings
- Adventurous paths to hidden beaches, perfect for exploring
- Playful approach to sustainability: counting turtles, exploring the organic farm, and more
- Golf cart safaris across the island are always full of surprises
- Sports and culture with the staff, genuine integration into island life
- Completely redesigned children's club

ACTIVITIES OFFERED AT THE RESORT:

- Private diving, snorkeling, fishing, stand-up paddle-boarding, and kayak trips
- Nature hikes through the lush jungle to lookout points and beaches
- Spa treatments and yoga sessions in the heart of nature
- Culinary delights in extraordinary places: nature picnics, beach dinners, and farm-to-table experiences
- Participation in nature conservation programs, bird watching, and sustainable farm projects
- Movie nights on the beach and cocktails at sunset in secluded spots

Left: When exploring the island with the Nature Conservation Manager you can marvel at turtles up close—always an impressive experience.

Above: On the go in a golf cart—the ideal way to explore the island's secrets, especially with young children.

WHY WE LOVE IT—OUR FAMILY EXPERIENCE:

Frégate cast its spell on us in a truly special way: exploring the island by golf cart, following winding paths to hidden bays and dreamlike beaches, encountering giant tortoises that roam the island like silent guardians, and the feeling of being part of a wonderful community. Nature Conservation Manager Anna Zora inspired us by introducing us to the island's rich flora and fauna, while our children delighted in feeding tortoises, snorkeling on the vibrant house reef, and discovering the organic farm with the gardener. We experienced Frégate as a place where closeness to nature and sustainability are not at odds with luxury; instead, they go hand in hand with it. Our villa hosts ensured that each day and every evening unfolded as a unique experience. From breakfast in our villa to picnics on hidden beaches, from cocktails at sunset atop the island's highest rock with ocean views, followed by candlelit dinners beneath the open sky—each of these impressive moments made us fall in love with Frégate a little more and we can hardly wait to see the "new" Frégate with our own eyes.

Above: The island boasts seven stunning beaches with the finest pearly white sand.

Right: Dedicated volunteers support the extensive nature conservation measures on Frégate Island—the island's impressive flora and fauna bear witness to their success.

ON NORTH ISLAND, DESERT ISLAND DREAMS BECOME REALITY: WILD BEACHES BETWEEN THE JUNGLE AND GRANITE PEAKS, WITH JUST ELEVEN ROMANTIC, LUXURIOUS VILLAS FAR FROM CIVILIZATION.

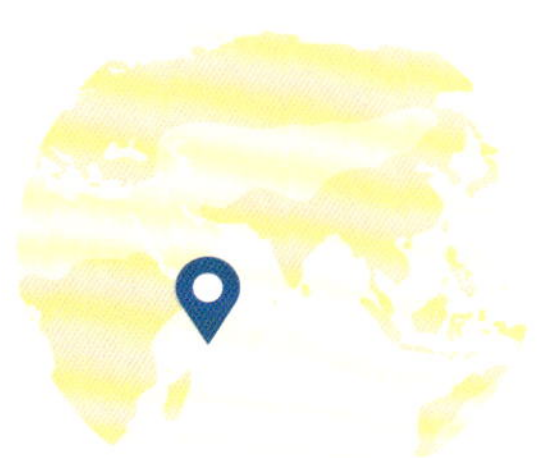

Where: Private island in the north of the Inner Seychelles, north of Madagascar in the Indian Ocean

What: Spacious villas on the long, sandy beach
Vibe: Secluded, luxurious, soft tourism

If Robinson Crusoe had been allowed to choose, he probably would have chosen this extraordinary corner of the world! As small as North Island may be at just two square kilometers on the outskirts of the Inner Seychelles, it has everything that defines the dream of a desert island: sparkling, fine, ivory-white sand, the shimmering turquoise and blue of the sea, and the lushest of greens!

RETURN TO A NATURAL PARADISE

Between swaying palm trees and the sound of the waves, there are just eleven spacious villas, all with their own pools. Tucked away along the beach, they are stylishly designed in an effortless feeling of luxury. The natural materials and airy architecture perfectly complement the island's wild charm. Used as a coconut plantation until a few decades ago, North Island is now allowed to flourish with its original biodiversity of flora and fauna once again. The rewilding concept has brought back giant tortoises and rare bird species. The soft tourism approach respects and supports nature conservation, offering the island as a peaceful refuge for all living things.
What makes North Island so unique is the freedom. Instead of fixed schedules, unique, tailor-made experiences are always available. Diving for the adults, movie nights on the beach for children, massages in the spa with breathtaking ocean views, and dinner in unusual locations prove anything is possible, and the service is so seamless that it never ceases to amaze. On North Island, every detail is deliberately special, embodying the art of simplicity.

NORTH ISLAND

Simply Beautiful

Previous page: Whether hiking in the mountains, taking boat trips, or simply relaxing at the beach bar—the breathtaking nature of North Island enhances every experience.

Below left: On guided nature adventures, children learn through play what it means to live with respect for nature.

Below right: Explore the secrets of remote bays on kayak tours.

ACTIVITIES OFFERED AT THE RESORT:

- Snorkeling and diving, stand-up paddleboarding, kayaking, fishing, and much more
- Guided hikes to secluded coves and up to the island's peak
- Spa treatments listening to the background sounds of nature and the ocean
- Yoga, meditation, and physical fitness take on a "desert island" character
- Individualized adventures: picnics and movies on the beach, sunsets in secret spots

HIGHLIGHTS FOR KIDS & TEENS:

- Personalized nature experiences: turtle watching, snorkeling, and fishing
- Guided family outings, each individually tailored to your needs, with activities for all ages
- Playfully discover and experience sustainability first-hand
- Abundant freedom, nature galore, no rigid itineraries—ideal for independent, curious children

WHY WE LOVE IT—OUR FAMILY EXPERIENCE:

An island with wild, white beaches, untamed nature, brimming with touching moments to be experienced—our childhood dreams came true for all of us here: witnessing tiny baby turtles hatch from the sand and plod towards the sea, meeting majestic giant tortoises, climbing Spa Hill with the whole family to experience the sublime beauty of the island from above ... It is and remains the unique combination of simplicity and abundance, of natural minimalism and perfect hospitality that makes North Island the most beautiful place on Earth for us!

Above: Everything in natural harmony—restaurant and idyllic beach in perfect symbiosis.

Left: Savor meals wherever you desire: private dining on your own terrace.

SIX SENSES ZIL PASYON

On a Blissful Beach

FÉLICITÉ LIVES UP TO ITS NAME AS THE SEYCHELLES' "ISLAND OF BLISS": THIS EXCLUSIVE RESORT OFFERS FREEDOM, TRANQUILITY, AND IMMERSIVE NATURE EXPERIENCES FOR ALL AGES.

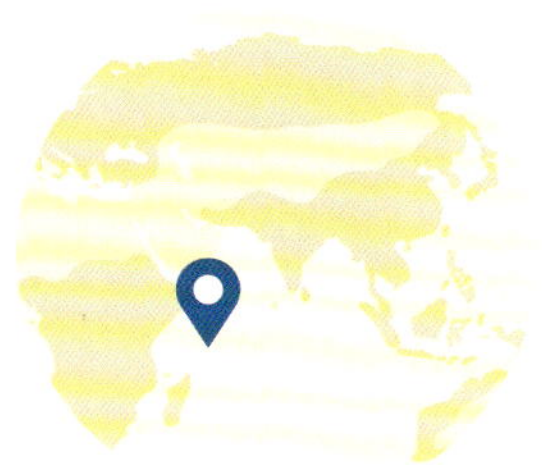

Where: Private island in the Inner Seychelles, north of Madagascar in the Indian Ocean

What: 30 villas and 3 residences, perched on rocks or surrounded by tropical vegetation
Vibe: Stylish, very close to nature, personalized

The landscape of the private Seychelles island of Félicité is breathtaking from the air. On the 20-minute helicopter flight from Mahé, the juxtaposition of lush jungle greenery, pearly white sand, and the multifaceted blues of the endless ocean is mesmerizing. Time and the elements have shaped the granite rocks that define the island into unique sculptures. In the 30 spacious villas and three residences—with up to four bedrooms—at Six Senses Zil Pasyon, the balance between modern architecture and the natural world has been masterfully achieved. Tucked away in the jungle or dramatically positioned on rocky plateaus, they are retreats that offer private refuge and awe-inspiring views that are especially spectacular from the private infinity pools!

The surrounding vegetation appears wild and untouched, thanks to the intensive efforts of the resort and environmental initiatives to restore the original biodiversity to this former plantation island. Sea turtles now feel at home here once again. If you are fortunate enough to be at Zil Pasyon when the eggs are laid or the tiny baby turtles hatch, it will be a heartwarming experience you will remember for the rest of your life. Whether you are exploring the jungle on guided hikes or paddling around the impressive rock formations in a kayak or on a stand-up paddleboard, you will realize that the flora and fauna are not just in the background; they are the stars of this island adventure.

HAPPINESS IS FOUND IN TRANQUILITY

Félicité means bliss, and that's exactly what you'll find here. Paths between palm trees lead to secluded sandy beaches. You can snorkel on the nearby reef while admiring the colorful underwater world. The sunsets, which you can witness high up on the rocky plateaus while enjoying a picnic with a fire pit, are breathtaking. Spa treatments harmonize with the elements and the restaurants and bars blend influences from Africa, Asia, and Europe. If you're interested, you can even take a cooking class. At Zil Pasyon, every family member is sure to find their bliss!

HIGHLIGHTS FOR KIDS & TEENS:

- Guided discovery tours around the island—both exciting and educational
- Nature experiences with plenty of freedom: watch baby turtles, go on treasure hunts, and much more
- Water adventures ranging from snorkeling excursions to kayak tours
- Children's cooking classes with fresh ingredients from the island's gardens
- Family movie nights in the open air

ACTIVITIES OFFERED AT THE RESORT:

- Private sunset dinners in hidden coves or overlooking the magnificent island landscape
- Treatments in a spa nestled strikingly among the rocks
- Sustainability programs, yoga classes, picnics, and boat trips to surrounding islands
- Snorkeling, diving, stand-up paddleboarding, and kayaking
- Guided hikes through the island's diverse landscapes

Left: Paddling a kayak through crystal-clear waters between the rocks allows you to experience nature's beauty from a new perspective.

Above: A fire pit picnic as the evening sky glows—creating memories that last forever.

The rocks on the sandy beach resemble sculptures formed by artists' hands.

Above: Some of the villas sit atop the smoothly polished rock plateaus, offering spectacular views.

Right: The resort island rises gently from the blue ocean.

WHY WE LOVE IT—OUR FAMILY EXPERIENCE:

What touched us so much about Zil Pasyon was the tranquility, this precious feeling of being completely in touch with yourself. It is a place that manages to be free of formality and dress codes—cool, casual, and yet always stylish. The dramatic rock formations lend an archaic character to the landscape. Enjoying our evening drinks on the rocks bathed in the glow of the evening light was unforgettable for all of us, with a fire pit, delicious snacks, and the incomparable feeling of the world standing still for a moment! The small cove below the resort also quickly became one of our favorite spots. Early in the morning, we snorkeled with our children in crystal-clear water, accompanied by exotic fish dancing around the coral. The kayak excursions to the surrounding islands were also fantastic—wild, quiet, and simply beautiful. We experienced Zil Pasyon as an island just for ourselves, a place that is both spectacular and yet filled with tranquility—which is precisely why it remains so deeply etched in our memories.

Above: The pool and bar invite you to enjoy a drink at sunset.

Right: Sometimes happiness looks like this—an elegant bathroom with panoramic windows and a swing.

SONEVA FUSHI

Barefoot in the Heart of a Luxury Paradise

SONEVA FUSHI IS HOME TO EXTRAORDINARY SIMPLICITY: DISCOVER THE LIGHTNESS OF BAREFOOT LUXURY—FREE, WILD, CREATIVE, AND CONNECTED TO NATURE'S TRUE RICHES.

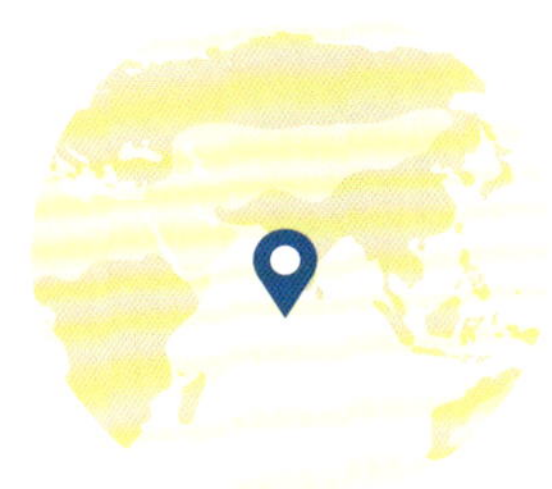

Where: A beautiful island in the Baa Atoll of the Maledives, UNESCO Biosphere Reserve in the Indian Ocean, southwest of Sri Lanka

What: Private villas nestled in lush jungle greenery, next to or right over the ocean

Vibe: Relaxed, light, and sustainable

The moment you step onto Soneva Fushi, fine sand underfoot, it feels as though you have arrived in paradise. The luxury of walking barefoot instantly reconnects us with carefree childhood days—perhaps this is the secret to letting go of everyday life? The Maldives are the dream destination for precisely this kind of relaxed escape and adventure. On a private island in the Baa Atoll, protected since 2011 as a UNESCO Biosphere Reserve, Soneva Fushi hides within tropical jungle greenery, an extraordinary resort that redefines the very notion of luxury. Your home away from home consists of select villas, stylishly and sustainably designed with natural materials that capture the lightness of the tropics. Whether nestled in emerald-green vegetation, set directly on the pearl-white beach, or perched on stilts above the lagoon's blue waters, each expansive villa brings you closer to nature—from sunrise to stargazing beneath the night sky. A zipline ride glides you straight into a gourmet restaurant perched high above the jungle canopy. Another fine-dining venue seems to float above the water, serving delicacies from the lagoon and the resort's organic garden. For those sweet indulgences, a chocolatier and ice cream parlor are always just a tempting moment away.

Dreamy film nights await in the open-air movie theater, while the observatory invites you to explore the night sky. At the glassblowing studio, guests can discover new talents through the art of upcycling—creating memories not only for children, but for the whole family to cherish.

CREATIVITY AND RESPECT FOR NATURE

Soneva Fushi embodies an incomparable way of life, defined by lightness, creativity, and a deep reverence for nature. Sustainability lives in every detail, from resource-saving solar power to rigorous zero-waste and recycling practices, to innovative coral protection using 3D-printed reef structures.

ACTIVITIES OFFERED AT THE RESORT:

- Snorkeling on the coral reef or diving with manta rays in Hanifaru Bay
- Spa experiences: Ayurveda, massages, sound therapy, and healing rituals
- Gourmet dining high above the jungle or in a restaurant on stilts over the ocean
- Yoga and meditation on the beach or in the spa pavilion
- Art workshops in the glassblowing studio
- Jungle hikes, dolphin tours, and picnics on deserted sandbanks
- Various courses, from cooking and padel tennis to surfing and diving adventures

HIGHLIGHTS FOR KIDS & TEENS:

- Children's club: Unmatched worldwide in size, variety, and attentive care, with music room, Lego lounge, pirate ship, and much more
- Eco Centro: At the resort's sustainable heart, children learn through play how recycling works and see that even trash has hidden value
- Sports & adventure: From bike tours and island explorations to a wide range of water activities (snorkeling, diving, kayaking, and more)
- Open-air movies under the stars right on the beach, "feet in the sand, popcorn in hand"
- Children's spa: Special pampering programs designed especially for younger guests

Left: Water adventures and Lego creativity await at the children's club.

Above: From sailing to deep diving to snorkeling, experienced guides lead the way through aquatic adventures.

Always in touch with nature: deliciousness on high in the treetop restaurant

Above: By boat to the secluded beaches and snorkeling tours on the reef

Right: A long jetty leads to the enchanting overwater restaurant

WHY WE LOVE IT—OUR FAMILY EXPERIENCE:

Hidden paths leading to the spa high above the jungle canopy, the friendly island rabbits our youngest son still talks about, barefoot morning rides on nostalgic bicycles through palm trees and exotic blossoms with the turquoise sea always in view—Soneva Fushi gave us space to breathe, inspired us, and set new standards for sustainable luxury. And then there was the breakfast, truly without equal. Like wandering through the marketplace, we strolled along the lavish buffet, choosing whatever our hearts desired, and moments later the warm-hearted staff freshly prepared it before artfully presenting it at our table. It was wonderful to watch our youngest play so happily in the children's club with the caring Maldivian staff, connecting as if they spoke the same language. Our older boys tried freediving for the first time, guided by experienced instructors who ensured their safety while sharing their passion for discovery. At Soneva Fushi, sustainability was not merely a concept but a way of life, and we treasured experiencing this paradise in true harmony with nature. It has become a place we long to return to as a family. We also fell in love with the expansive villas, each uniquely crafted from island materials—and where else can you slip straight from your bedroom into your own private pool?

Above: The largest of the private villas—almost a village in itself.

Right: Some houses have their own water slides leading directly into the crystal-clear water.

SONEVA JANI

Floating Between Sky and Sea

SONEVA JANI: WHERE EVERYDAY LIFE MELTS AWAY AND LUXURY MEETS PLAYFUL NATURALNESS—EXPLORE WITH WONDER, RELAX COMPLETELY, SIMPLY BE.

Opposite page: The villas at Soneva Jani appear to float above the water.

Above: The children's club is nestled in the island's jungle.

Right: Cycling across the island and out onto the lagoon.

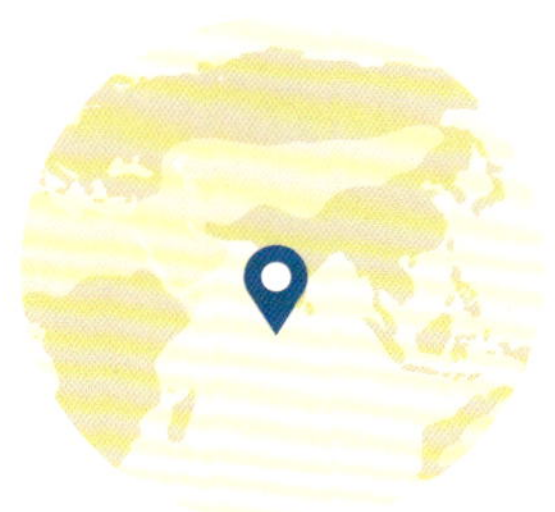

Where: Private island in the southern tip of the Maldives' Noonu Atoll, in the Indian Ocean southwest of Sri Lanka

What: Spacious villas over the ocean or on the beach
Vibe: Expansive, natural, relaxed, and playful

Each water villa has a slide leading from the upper floor directly into the lagoon.

Opposite page: Climbing on the pirate ship, a game of air hockey, or billiards with a view over the treetops—the children's club also appeals to teenagers.

Wooden walkways wind across the lagoon's blue expanse, as elegantly as a delicate coral formation. Individual villas, seemingly floating above the water, line up like pearls on a string. Soneva Jani is indeed a true jewel. With just 51 water villas and ten beach villas, this resort in the Noonu Atoll offers precisely the privacy families dream of in a tropical paradise. Every spacious villa, crafted entirely in natural wood, opens onto wide horizons, with sweeping views from the sun deck and the villa's own "floating" pool. By night, nothing rivals gazing at the stars when the retractable roof over the bedroom slides back. And in the morning, who could resist starting the day by gliding down the waterslide straight into the warm lagoon? It is a dream come true for children and adults alike!

SUSTAINABLE CONCEPT AND UNIQUE EXPERIENCES

Beyond the villas, this barefoot-luxury resort has even more to offer. Sports of every kind await on and under the water; on land, padel tennis is played amidst lush greenery, and the island's long, slender shape is perfect for family bike rides.

The name Soneva Jani comes from the Sanskrit expression for "wisdom," and this philosophy shapes the entire resort. Sustainability and respect for nature go hand in hand with freedom and well-being. Snorkeling tours with marine biologists, eco-inspired art workshops, adventures and creativity in the children's club (where even teenagers have fun), wellness in the midst of tropical greenery, or movies in the lagoon under the stars—the uniqueness of each experience takes center stage.

The same applies to the cuisine. Explore gourmet dishes in the organic garden, enjoy a sunset dinner in overwater restaurants, or sway in hanging chairs at the beach hut while being served fresh-caught seafood. Every detail is designed so that children and parents alike feel relaxed and cared for.

HIGHLIGHTS FOR KIDS & TEENS:

- Children's club: Along with the pool playground and pirate ship climbing area, kids will find billiards, digital creative spaces, a movie theater, and much more
- Waterslides straight from your private villa—a true highlight for children and parents alike
- Discover sustainability playfully with coral-protection workshops
- Floating silent open-air movie theater under the stars
- Dolphin-watching and snorkeling with marine biologists offer an introduction to the lagoon's wonders

ACTIVITIES OFFERED AT THE RESORT:

- Sports on and under the water: kayaking, stand-up paddling, windsurfing, or snorkeling and diving with marine biologists on the biodiverse house reef
- Sunrise picnic on a deserted sandbank, dinner in the organic garden, wine cellar tastings, not to mention ice cream and chocolate creations all day long
- Ayurveda, yoga, sound therapy, and treatments in spa pavilions set amid the lagoon
- Discover the tropical night sky at the overwater observatory—hands-on science for all ages

WHY WE LOVE IT—OUR FAMILY EXPERIENCE:

What captivated us most at Soneva Jani was the sense of space: the endless horizon stretching across the sea, the long cycling routes gliding over the lagoon's wooden walkways or pedaling on jungle paths to hidden bays ... and the sense of spaciousness in every respect. Everything simply fit together perfectly! Our villa quickly became our favorite refuge. While the children shot down our own waterslide again and again, plunging from the upper floor straight into the lagoon, we savored the island's lightness, coffee in hand and feet in the pool. Culinary pleasures mirrored this effortless lifestyle, none more memorable than freshly grilled crab in the romantic beach hut, accompanied by chilled rosé and the gentle sounds of the lagoon. We were especially impressed by the children's club, embraced even by our teenagers without feeling too old for it. With its own area for chilling, musical instruments, and digital tools for filmmaking, coding, and music production, it inspired without trying too hard.

THE NAUTILUS MALDIVES

Go with the Flow

A SECLUDED, DREAMY ISLAND WITH JUST A HANDFUL OF RESIDENCES BETWEEN PALM TREES AND OCEAN, WITH COMPLETE FREEDOM TO FOLLOW YOUR HEART: THE NAUTILUS REDEFINES LUXURY.

Where: Intimate private island in the heart of the Maldives' Baa Atoll, a UNESCO biosphere reserve in the Indian Ocean southwest of Sri Lanka

What: Spacious residences on the beach or in the lagoon
Vibe: Bespoke luxury with absolute privacy and a keen commitment to individuality

The gentle rhythm of the waves acts as a soundtrack to the easy tempo and distinct feeling of freedom that characterizes the luxurious island world of The Nautilus. There are just 26 houses and residences here, some on the beach and some over the lagoon, all with generously spacious designs and furnished with private pools. Organic shapes, natural materials, and an ultra-luxurious bohemian style that features playful splashes of color—perfectly elegant ways to enjoy everything in blissful privacy and personalized comfort. These luxury residences bring to mind the shells of the underwater world surrounding its visitors. The biodiverse house reef practically begins at the very edge of your terrace, and the ledge of the reef, home to fish, corals, and even the occasional turtle, is always just a short swim away. A few steps across the fine sand and children can snorkel and splash around in the clear, shallow water—that is, unless they are busy having fun in the children's club. The older children can paddle stand-up paddleboards and explore the underwater world with marine biologists, while their parents relax by the pool and enjoy canapés and cocktails.
The adventures continue on the resort's luxury yachts. You may choose to take a sunset cruise with a gourmet picnic on a secluded sandbank, or a day trip to dive and watch manta rays in world-famous Hanifaru Bay. Or you can simply enjoy the vastness of the blue ocean from the deck of the yacht, because after all, true luxury is the ability to experience everything exactly as you desire.

ENDLESS OPTIONS, NO OBLIGATIONS

In this timeless paradise, freedom defines everyday life. Here, endless possibilities await you; menus serve only as inspiration, dress codes are forgotten, and you have round-the-clock service at your disposal. Breakfast in the afternoon, dinner on your private sun deck or in a romantic candlelight setting on the beach, a spa treatment in the middle of the night, a private sailing trip—this island offers boundless opportunities for both children and parents to relax and unwind.

Previous pages: Indulgence above the water in a spectacular restaurant location.

Opposite page: Splash about and enjoy refreshments around the clock at the pool lounge.

Below left: Luxurious villas with generous open spaces and private pools serve as oases for relaxation for the whole family.

Below right: The Nautilus offers plenty of variety for children, from pirate adventures with the children's club to fascinating workshops and fun on the beach.

HIGHLIGHTS FOR KIDS & TEENS:

- Children's club with friendly staff and personalized activities, from pirate adventures to cooking lessons, along with lots of creative fun
- Snorkeling with marine biologists and microscopy workshops that show the importance of protecting the oceans
- Family movie time on the beach with fresh popcorn under starry skies
- Child-friendly massages and wellness treatments in the spa

ACTIVITIES OFFERED AT THE RESORT:

- Snorkeling and diving on the house reef or in world-famous Hanifaru Bay, in the heart of the UNESCO Biosphere Reserve
- Breakfast at sunset? Picnic on the yacht? Indulge yourself whenever and wherever you wish
- Holistic treatments, yoga, and meditation in the overwater spa
- Kayaking, stand-up paddleboarding, wakeboarding, paddle tennis & more, including private sailing trips and dolphin-watching outings
- Mixology workshop, Maldivian cooking courses, and underwater photography

WHY WE LOVE IT—OUR FAMILY EXPERIENCE:

For us, The Nautilus was the epitome of slowing down. Everything felt so free and easy—no set times, no deadlines, no obligations. Instead, there emerged that special flow that is all too often missing in everyday life with children. I'll never forget the evening movie on the beach: the gentle lapping of the ocean, the sky full of stars, and all of us, not just the children, sitting barefoot on the sand watching the movie with sparkling eyes and eating fresh popcorn. With its blend of colorful design, maximum privacy, and genuine freedom, The Nautilus has mastered the art of being ultra-luxurious yet utterly approachable.

COMO MAALIFUSHI

Discovering Simplicity

AN ISLAND WORLD WHERE PEACEFUL TRANQUILITY MEETS ENCHANTING CORAL REEFS, COMBINING PERFECTION WITH NATURALNESS: THIS RESORT WINS HEARTS BY REMAINING REFRESHINGLY UNPRETENTIOUS.

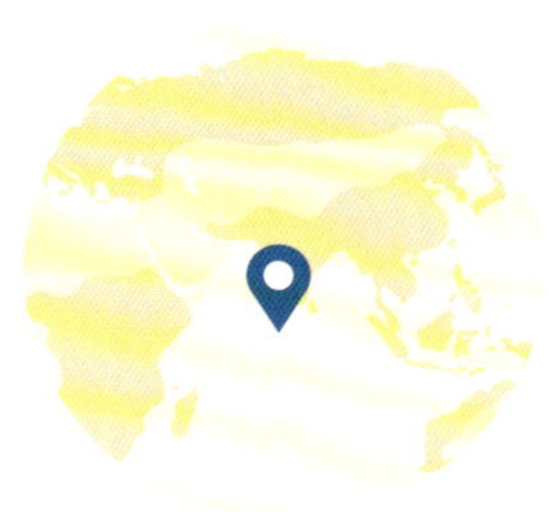

Where: The private island of Maalifushi in the remote Thaa Atoll, located in the southern part of the Maldives

What: Spacious, stylish, beachside and overwater villas
Vibe: Pure and peaceful, centered on conscious experiences

Combining simplicity, clarity, and a natural state of being with luxury is an art that Como Maalifushi has mastered. Everything feels light, and you are constantly in harmony with nature. The resort chose the perfect location for this—the virtually untouched Thaa Atoll in the south of the Maldives. Its 59 villas ensure complete privacy, whether they are on the beach, surrounded by lush tropical vegetation, or elegantly perched on a jetty above the crystal-clear waters. Despite the resort's luxury amenities, there is an absence of pomp and grandeur. Instead, the focus is on simplicity and authenticity. The stylishly sleek villa furnishings bear the signature of a renowned Japanese designer, while the understated architecture blends harmoniously into the tropical jungle and lagoon. You can experience mindfulness and closeness to nature in the tranquility of the spa, which follows the Shambhala philosophy, and throughout the varied cuisine, which combines gourmet pleasure with the pursuit of well-being.

Every meal is an experience: from a "floating" breakfast in your private pool to a Maldivian meal on the beach, listening to the sound of the waves. If you want to experience the feeling of landing on a remote island paradise far from civilization, you can picnic on a secluded sandbank and even spend the night under the stars, indulging in Robinson Crusoe-inspired solitude.

EXPERIENCE THE OCEAN WITH ALL YOUR SENSES

The ocean, rich in biodiversity, is ever-present in the resort's activities. Water sports for active visitors and opportunities to explore the Maldives' aquatic world are tailored to the whole family. You can have your first snorkeling adventures right on your doorstep, enjoy dolphin-watching boat tours, and go on reef dives accompanied by marine biologists, where you can observe turtles amid colorful corals and tropical fish.

HIGHLIGHTS FOR KIDS & TEENS:

- A variety of activities at the children's club, with a relaxed atmosphere and charming Scandinavian-style furnishings
- Spot dolphins on boat tours or get splashed by the waves in the boom net
- Explore underwater life on playful snorkeling safaris
- Learn about and prepare healthy treats in child-friendly cooking workshops
- Imaginative treasure hunts and new beach games daily for children eager to keep moving

ACTIVITIES OFFERED AT THE RESORT:

- Snorkeling and diving on one of the best-preserved house reefs in the Maldives
- Watersports including surfing, stand-up paddle-boarding, kayaking, wakeboarding, and more
- Overwater spa sanctuary for yoga, massages, and treatments
- Maldivian, Asian-international, or Ayurvedic-influenced Shambhala cuisine
- Individual experiences: dolphin-watching boat trips, island hopping, and picnicking on a secluded sandbank
- Visit an island and meet the local people

Left: On a dolphin-spotting boat trip.

Top and above: Encountering turtles while snorkeling with marine biologists and picnicking on a secluded sandbank—experiences that create lasting memories.

Above left: One of the coral reef's most remarkable inhabitants—the blue-striped fangblenny.

Above right: A place of serenity—the spa is inspired by the Shambhala philosophy.

Left: Enjoying life under the palms—poolside dining overlooking the lagoon.

WHY WE LOVE IT—OUR FAMILY EXPERIENCE:

Como Maalifushi was a very special place for us: quiet, yet powerful and unforgettable. It starts with the design: white, light wood and wonderfully airy. This creates an atmosphere of quiet confidence—no gimmicks, no rushing, just pure feeling. Our youngest immediately felt at home in the children's club with its warm wood tones and friendly supervision. One of the most magical moments, where everything aligned perfectly, was the dolphin-watching trip. We had barely begun gliding through the water on the boom net with our feet in the water and refreshing spray on our faces when a small pod of dolphins appeared right next to us—as if they had sensed our wide-eyed wonder! The culinary experiences were as light and relaxed for all members of the family as the special spa experience: Yoga with an ocean view, accompanied by the gentle rustling of palm trees, was not a quest for perfection, but a return to what really matters. Although Como Maalifushi doesn't set out to impress its guests, it does so all the more—in a deeply touching way that lingers long in memory.

Above: Its palm tree islands and organic shapes help the pool's landscape blend into its natural surroundings.

Right: Wellness for every generation—even toddlers enjoy family yoga.

Art and Creation

ARTFUL DESIGN, EFFORTLESS NATURE: IN THIS PRIVATE ISLAND WORLD, SPACE ABOUNDS FOR PERSONAL DISCOVERY: CULTURE, CUISINE, WATER SPORTS, WELLNESS—EACH DAY IS A NEW WORK OF ART!.

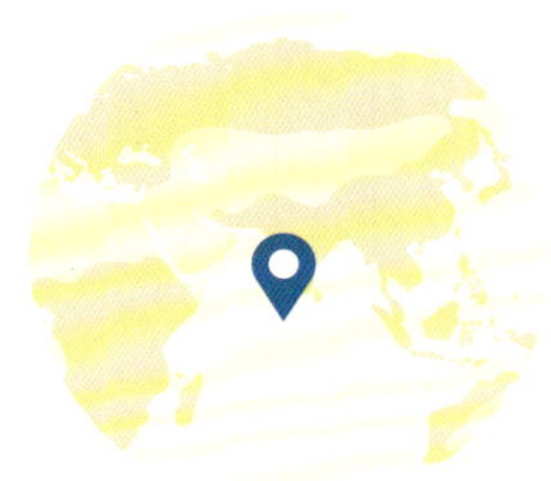

Where: Fari Islands in the North Malé Atoll of the Maldives, in the Indian Ocean southwest of Sri Lanka

What: Spacious, elegantly furnished designer villas
Vibe: Balanced, relaxing, and inspiring

Left: The stylish Fari Beach Club—a cool look in warm colors.

Opposite page (top left, center, right): Whether dining on the beach or gazing into the distance from your villa's deck, the ocean is a constant companion.

Opposite page, bottom: The permaculture garden also doubles as a restaurant. The entire resort operates on the zero-waste principle.

HIGHLIGHTS FOR KIDS & TEENS:

- Children's club with nature projects, 3D printing, Formula 1 Model Block, and plenty of space for playful creativity
- Hands-on workshops ranging from recycling projects to painting
- Memorable family experiences including snorkeling, dolphin watching, and picnics on a sandbank

ACTIVITIES OFFERED AT THE RESORT:

- Diving and snorkeling on guided excursions with marine biologists
- Boat trips and water sports
- Morning beach yoga, meditation, spa treatments, and personal training
- A dozen restaurants and bars, from elegant fine dining to relaxed beach clubs
- Galleries, design boutiques, and cultural events at Fari Marina
- Sustainable experiences, such as eco-projects at the coral reef and in the permaculture garden

The spacious villas offer plenty of open-air space yet a great deal of privacy.

The Fari Islands are a marvel of creativity on many levels. First and foremost, because this archipelago of four islands, one of which is home to Patina resort, was created entirely by human hands. Just a 45-minute speedboat ride from Malé Airport, it is hard to believe that just a few years ago this lush, spacious landscape of vegetation and beaches was nothing more than a solitary sandbank.

Patina, with 90 villas and 20 studios, embodies an innovative resort concept: Minimalist design by a celebrated Brazilian architect meets a conscious approach to resources. Interiors are defined by natural materials and a calming aesthetic.

EXCLUSIVE CULTURAL PROGRAM

Sculptures and installations by renowned artists turn every stroll into an inspiring journey. Creative workshops and a carefully curated mix of events, wellness programs, and family activities make for a richly varied vacation approach. Guests choose how to experience island life: peacefully in their own villa with its private pool and sweeping ocean views, or in the lively hub of Fari Marina, with its boutiques, galleries, bars, and performance venues. From here, it is just a short boat ride to neighboring resorts, where restaurants and spas welcome Patina guests. Patina has mastered the art of offering diversity without being overwhelming. Water activities range from surfing and snorkeling to dives in a mini-submarine. The children's club focuses on sports, with soccer camps that top European clubs even take advantage of. Over a dozen culinary concepts from food trucks and slow food in the garden restaurant to sunset dinners on the beach and sleek designer bars make every meal an event.

Above left: Breakfast bliss not only for young foodies.

Above right: The library is a stylish room offering tranquility.

Right: Colorful and delicious—the ice cream cart right on the beach

WHY WE LOVE IT—OUR FAMILY EXPERIENCE:

It is this blend of clarity and atmosphere, of design and emotion, that makes Patina so special. The interplay of sustainability, innovative architecture, and a strong focus on art feels seamless and authentic, never contrived. Art plays a quiet yet ever-present role. Every piece along the path invites you to look more closely and feel more deeply. What struck us most was the freedom to shape each day differently—retreating to the privacy of our villa, immersing ourselves in the vibrant energy of the marina, or simply taking a boat to a neighboring resort's spa or restaurant. Patina also impressed us with its culinary innovation: urban-style gourmet dining alongside colorful food trucks, an ice cream cart on the beach, and even a thoughtfully composed breakfast enjoyed in our own pool. And just like our son was captivated by the soccer camp at the children's club, every member of our family found the freedom to flourish here in their own way.

VELAA

VELAA PRIVATE ISLAND

All the World's a Stage

VELAA PRIVATE ISLAND HAS IT ALL, WITHOUT COMPROMISE: THIS PREMIER MALDIVIAN RESORT EXCELS IN SPORTS ACTIVITIES, SOPHISTICATED DESIGN, AND EXCLUSIVITY, SHOWCASING PERFECTION AT EVERY TURN.

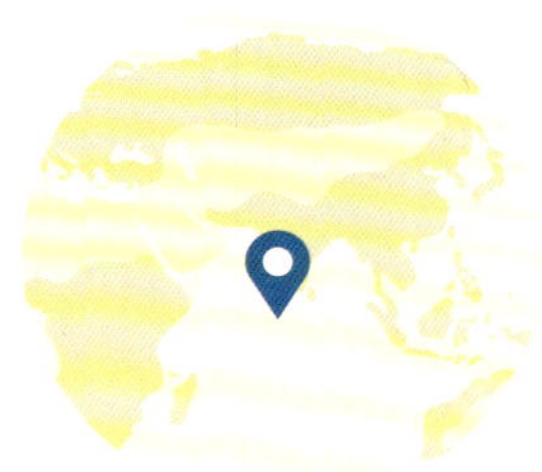

Where: Private island in the Noonu Atoll of the Maldives, southwest of Sri Lanka in the Indian Ocean

What: Around 50 luxury villas and residences
Vibe: Uncompromisingly luxurious, spectacular, and extravagant

You could almost believe that Velaa Private Island is not an island, but a gigantic stage—reserved for the most special of moments! The resort orchestrates a spectacular luxury vacation, with pomp and pageantry and entertainment from morning to night. And yet, nothing feels artificial here, thoughtfully executed down to the very last detail.
In the heart of the Noonu Atoll, Velaa has created a world of its own that allows you to retreat into privacy while still enjoying an extroverted vacation atmosphere. Even the concept of privacy can be taken to the extreme here if desired. Some of the 50 flawlessly designed residences are only accessible by boat, enabling complete solitude without sacrificing any amenities. A private pool and round-the-clock personal butler service, as discreet and prompt as it is personal, seem like a matter of course here.

TOP-CLASS CHILD CARE

Everything is possible, except for one thing—having to go without. From French haute cuisine to Asian fusion cuisine—served without equal in a restaurant tower with one of the most extensive wine cellars the region has to offer—to a spa sanctuary over the water, everything is within reach. The children's club is, of course, no exception. It offers a wide range of activities with its creative program and water park, and the youngsters are warmly welcomed by their caregiver the moment they arrive.

The fact that a Maldives resort offers water sports ranging from snorkeling to stand-up paddleboarding tours is fairly typical. At Velaa, you'll also find an element of the atypical, of the extraordinary. Cutting-edge equipment such as eFoil surfboards, seabobs, jet skis, and flyboards will fascinate even well-traveled thrill-seekers. On land, you will find a high-tech gym, a covered tennis court, a climbing wall, a soccer pitch, and even a nine-hole golf course.

Previous page: Some of the villas are only accessible by boat and offer maximum privacy.

Opposite page: The interiors of the accommodations combine modern design with regional elements.

Below left and bottom: High-tech water sports—eFoil surfing and whizzing through crystal-clear waters on a seabob.

Below right: Velaa Private Island even boasts a nine-hole golf course.

HIGHLIGHTS FOR KIDS & TEENS:

- Spacious children's club with its own water park and an activity-packed program
- Tennis, soccer, and water sports for children
- Spa services, cooking experiences, and open-air movies—all designed with children in mind
- Nature discovery tours, treasure hunts, and mini island adventures
- Personal supervision—flexible and imaginative

ACTIVITIES OFFERED AT THE RESORT:

- Professional sports: nine-hole golf course, tennis, diving, and more
- Two covered padel courts with lessons for beginners and pros
- High-tech water action: seabobs, jet skiing, flyboarding, eFoil surfing, and a variety of additional activities
- Dolphin-watching trips and sunset cruises listening to the sounds of nature
- Gourmet experiences in multiple restaurants plus an impressive wine cellar
- Spa, yoga, personal training, and physical fitness—all customized for you
- Evening entertainment with live shows and fireworks

WHY WE LOVE IT—OUR FAMILY EXPERIENCE:

Velaa celebrates life—perhaps more elegantly than elsewhere, certainly louder, but in the very best way: evening shows, music, and twinkling lights infuse glamour into the tranquility that lies over the vast ocean. With its extraordinary extravagance, a range of sports that we found amazing, and perfection in every detail, the island took our breath away: golf on the designer golf course, padel tennis, whizzing through the lagoon on a seabob—a multitude of impressions that remain with us, despite the fact that we are more accustomed to a quieter atmosphere.

Fairytale Beauty by Crystal-Clear Waters

FIVE HISTORIC TEA PLANTATION BUNGALOWS OFFER LUXURIOUS RETREATS IN SRI LANKA'S FABULOUSLY BEAUTIFUL HIGHLAND VALLEYS—A WORLD OF QUIETLY ENDURING EXPERIENCES.

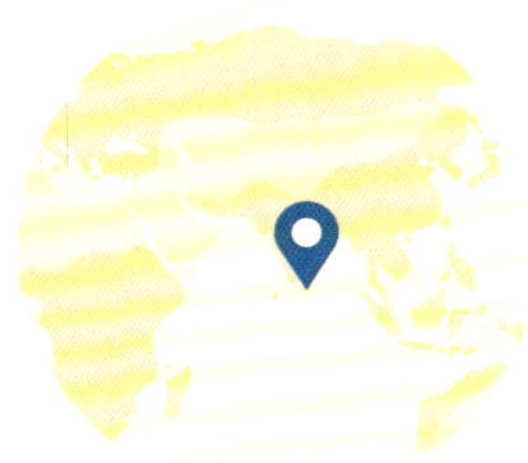

Where: Surrounding Castlereagh Reservoir in Sri Lanka's mountainous Central Highlands, a designated UNESCO World Heritage Site

What: 5 restored bungalows from the colonial era, each with a few suites
Vibe: Elegant, quiet, with a nostalgic flair

A stay at Ceylon Tea Trails in Sri Lanka's highlands is like stepping back in time. Nestled in the rolling hills of the UNESCO World Heritage region, surrounding Castlereagh Reservoir, lies a collection of five historic bungalows. Each has its own history and individual style; sometimes elegant, sometimes a bit rustic, but all authentic. The vistas over the tea plantations are magical, especially in the early hours of the morning, when a gentle mist drifts through the highland valley and the first rays of sunlight cast a golden glow across the emerald slopes.

TIME-HONORED BUILDINGS, STYLISH LUXURY

Former residences of tea planters, these bungalows have been lavishly restored, each offering a small number of suites. Elegant period furniture and attentive yet never intrusive service conjure the noblesse of a bygone age. In the intimate atmosphere of the drawing room, library, and dining room, guests feel less like travelers in a hotel and more like they are enjoying a relaxing visit with good friends.

Life in the nostalgic world of Ceylon Tea Trails follows its own rhythm. Mornings begin with an exquisite breakfast on the veranda, while afternoons feature a classic ritual of tea in the garden, complete with British sandwiches and scones. In the evening, gourmet dinners are prepared with the finest regional ingredients and tailored to personal tastes. For those who seek relaxation, wellness treatments can be enjoyed in the quiet comfort of one's own suite.

Active guests will find a wealth of experiences at Ceylon Tea Trails. Meander along old plantation paths, discover the secrets behind the incomparable flavor of Ceylon tea on a guided tea factory visit, explore the beautiful landscape with its small mountain villages by bike, or enjoy the tranquility of the lake by boat. The unhurried atmosphere of Ceylon Tea Trails, a sister lodge of Wild Coast Tented and Cape Weligama, lingers long after the journey ends.

Previous pages: The Central Highlands of Sri Lanka with their lush vegetation, home to Ceylon Tea Trails.

Opposite page: Colorful tuk-tuks are a common sight on the narrow roads of the hill country.

The bungalows are nestled in wonderful garden landscapes.

Below left and bottom: Private whirlpool with a unique view. Arriving by seaplane—what a great adventure!

Below right: A boat trip on Castlereagh Reservoir offers new views of the landscape.

HIGHLIGHTS FOR KIDS & TEENS:

- Discover how tea is produced at the Junior Tea Planter Workshop, explained in a clear and age-appropriate manner
- Tennis at Tientsin, nature walks, and breakfast picnics
- Plenty of space to play outside in the gardens around the bungalows
- Relaxed dining: family-friendly menus at flexible times

ACTIVITIES OFFERED AT THE RESORT:

- Guided hikes through the tea plantations, along mountain trails, and past gorgeous viewpoints
- All about tea: tastings, guided tours, and talks with tea masters
- Nature walks, mountain bike tours on the tea trails, and kayaking on the lake
- Individual spa treatments and private yoga sessions
- Spectacular views: by helicopter or seaplane through the highlands

WHY WE LOVE IT—OUR FAMILY EXPERIENCE:

We fell in love with the serene beauty of Ceylon Tea Trails from the moment our seaplane swept over the lush green hills and touched down on the mirrored waters of the lake. In the historic bungalows, you have a feeling of complete seclusion. Our favorite spot was the hot tub on the terrace, offering endless views of the lake and mountains. Wonderful hiking trails through the tea plantations started right outside our front door. Visiting the tea factory, we felt the deep pride in a craft produced here for generations. We all found ourselves in awe on the boat tour across the tranquil Castlereagh Reservoir.

Luxury Wilderness Adventure

WHERE JUNGLE MEETS OCEAN AND GLAMPING MEETS EXTRAVAGANCE: WILD COAST TENTED LODGE IS AN EXTRAORDINARY CAMP COMBINING BOLD DESIGN WITH SAFARI-STYLE NATURE EXPERIENCES.

Where: On the southern coast of Sri Lanka near Yala National Park, where the jungle and ocean converge

What: Luxurious suites in cocoon-like tented buildings
Vibe: Variety, surrounded by nature with fantastic cuisine

Although the combination of national park, safari, and camping in the monsoon forest doesn't necessarily conjure images of a luxury resort, Wild Coast Tented Lodge successfully combines nature adventures with all the amenities that make a family vacation truly outstanding. The extraordinary architecture alone reveals a fundamentally different approach and the courage to implement a sustainable concept. Each suite is an organically shaped tent with views of the water or the lush greenery. These oversized cocoons offer interiors that are meticulously designed in a modern safari style, with heavenly beds and all the technological comforts you could wish for. The private pool on the terrace deck makes it undeniable: Wild Coast Tented Lodge is so much more than glamping!

ADVENTURES IN THE WILD

The experiences for children and for parents are specifically selected to suit individual interests. In the Junior Ranger program, children and teenagers learn about the importance of sustainability and protecting nature in a playful way. Guided nature walks and safaris offer exciting encounters with flora and fauna for the whole family.

The directly adjacent Yala National Park, the oldest nature reserve in Sri Lanka, is known for its diverse vegetation, dramatic coastlines, and impressive wildlife. It is home to elephants, sloth bears, crocodiles, blue peacocks, and much more. And you will find yourself completely mesmerized when one of the 30 or so leopards makes an appearance in the wild! As the best time for exciting safari experiences is in the early morning hours, children can look forward to having fun in the lodge's enormous free-form swimming pool afterwards while their parents spend time enjoying a treatment in the spa.

Wild Coast Tented Lodge also has a passion for indulgence. Private dinners on the beach, afternoon tea in the jungle, seafood in the elegant lodge dome—the culinary adventures that combine Sri Lankan and international flavors are equally exceptional.

HIGHLIGHTS FOR KIDS & TEENS:

- Family safari with outings in a semi-open jeep
- Junior Ranger program: Individual nature discoveries with rangers, such as tracking, family game drives, and a children's cooking course with a typical Sri Lankan dessert
- Beach walks and time at the pool to relax after the safari
- Creative workshops with natural materials and cooking over a fire

WHY WE LOVE IT – OUR FAMILY EXPERIENCE:

It was this unique contrast between rugged coastline and lush greenery, between leopards and lagoon, that left such a deep impression on us in Yala National Park. Wild Coast Tented Lodge captures Sri Lanka's diversity perfectly—thoughtfully designed, with bold style, its own untamed energy, and a keen sense for the extraordinary. Mornings were spent on safari, encountering leopards, and in the evenings we sat contentedly by the Indian Ocean, our feet in the sand and a glass in hand. Every moment felt like we were experiencing a completely different, yet always authentic, Sri Lanka.

Left, top to bottom: Tented cocoons with impressively equipped suites and extensive beach walks provide the deluxe safari experience!

Right, top to bottom: The landscape of the pool is magnificent! The organic architecture of the spacious main lodge echoes the colors and shapes of its natural surroundings.

A Garden of Paradise High Above the Ocean

A HAVEN OF SERENITY IN THE HEART OF ONE OF THE LIVELIEST SURFING HOTSPOTS ON SRI LANKA'S SOUTHERN COAST: CAPE WELIGAMA SEAMLESSLY BLENDS LUSH TROPICAL GARDENS, AUTHENTICITY, AND HIGH STANDARDS.

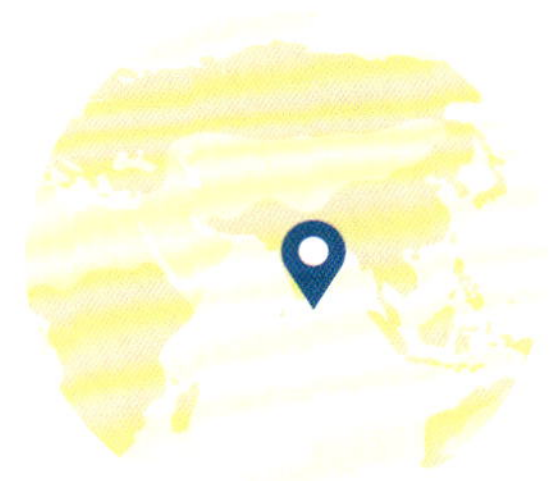

Where: West of the southernmost point of Sri Lanka, 150 km (95 miles) from the capital city of Colombo

What: 23 villas and 16 suites in terraced gardens
Vibe: With local flair and personalized service

Surrounded by rustling coconut palm trees, Cape Weligama gazes out over the endless azure of the Indian Ocean. Individually designed villas nestle around elegant pools in lush terraced gardens, giving the refreshingly green resort a village-like charm. Each secluded private residence boasts boundless views across the horizon. The spacious villas and suites are decorated in natural colors and with an understated style, offering every possible comfort—classic elegance harmonizes with local influences. This meticulous attention to detail extends to the personal service, which immediately makes guests feel at home. The expansive pool area adjacent to the suites is designed with families in mind, ensuring everyone feels comfortable and even the youngest guests can splash and play to their heart's content. At the outermost edge of the gardens, the crescent-shaped infinity pool high above the cliffs beckons with unsurpassed panoramic views of the majestic ocean—perfect for unwinding during the day and enjoying the sunset in the evening.

SURF, ENJOY, RELAX

The gentle ocean breeze infuses each day with a sense of lightness, inviting guests to go on outings to the coastal town of Galle and its historic fort, visit tea plantations and temples, and explore colorful markets and idyllic beaches at the base of the striking reddish cliffs. The wide, shallow bay of Weligama is perfect for surfing and boogie boarding, and those new to the sport can take their first surfing lessons on the beach.

Alongside international gourmet cuisine, Cape Weligama serves authentic island dishes that capture the true essence of Sri Lanka—unadulterated, flavorful, and fresh. Whether you're savoring breakfast on the terrace, enjoying a sunset drink by the pool, or strolling through the gardens in anticipation of being pampered at the resort's restaurants, Cape Weligama offers the perfect setting to experience southern Sri Lanka in style—relaxed, refined, and with a warm, family-friendly atmosphere.

Above: Just a few steps lead from the lush greenery of the gardens to the golden sands of the beach.

Right: Tropical gardens with ocean views—Cape Weligama's spectacular setting alone beckons visitors.

Above left: The crescent-shaped pool is bathed in unparalleled evening light.

Above right: Sri Lanka's wildlife never fails to fascinate.

Right: Guests enjoy sweeping ocean views from the elegant lounge chairs on the beach.

WHY WE LOVE IT—OUR FAMILY EXPERIENCE:

When we think back to Cape Weligama, we always picture the ocean. Whether we were sitting by the pool, having breakfast on the deck, or strolling through the gardens, our gaze was drawn to the ever-present expanse of the majestic and calming Indian Ocean. The architecture left a lasting impression as well. The individually designed villas are nestled in a lush green garden oasis, where everything feels open yet still private. We felt the attention to detail everywhere, from the warm welcome and attentive, personal service to the sophisticated design. The elegant and inviting lobby and restaurant greeted us in a vibrant blue and warm golden yellow reminiscent of a feast of exotic spices. Cape Weligama's culinary prowess was equally striking. Alongside global gourmet cuisine, we savored delicious dishes that tasted unmistakably of Sri Lanka. For us, it is a wonderful place where all the senses come alive and every stay creates space for unforgettable memories, like our extraordinary whale-watching catamaran cruise.

HIGHLIGHTS FOR KIDS & TEENS:

- Family-friendly pool area and infinity pool with views over the ocean
- Boogie boarding and surfing lessons for beginners right on the beach
- Birdwatching walks, local fish stall visits, and sea safaris with the in-house naturalist
- Discover Sri Lankan cuisine in family cooking classes
- Spacious villas and relaxed service; everything is designed to be child-friendly
- Cape Forest Camp—a five-day nature camp featuring creative courses and nature experiences with friendly staff

ACTIVITIES OFFERED AT THE RESORT:

- Infinity pool with spectacular ocean views
- Discover Sri Lankan cuisine experiences, cycling adventures in the South, and mask-painting lessons
- A variety of day trips: to Galle, tea plantations, or nearby national parks
- Experience the ocean: surfing, snorkeling, and seasonal whale watching
- Wellness and yoga overlooking the ocean
- Private dining on the cliffs or in your own garden pavilion

Above: At Cape Forest Camp, children enjoy an exciting mix of creative workshops and nature exploration.

Right: Hidden coves can be found just next to the resort grounds.

On the Edge of the Wild

A CONVERSATION WITH CHRIS BURCH ABOUT NIHI SUMBA AND THE POWER OF A GENUINE CONNECTION WITH PEOPLE AND THE LOCAL CULTURE.

Q: *Mr. Burch, you have found a kind of second home on Sumba. What does this island mean to you personally?*
A: To me, Sumba is the most beautiful place in the world. When I first came here, there was only a small surf hotel at Nihiwatu Beach in untouched surroundings. I immediately knew this place was something truly special. My three sons are enthusiastic surfers and were the reason for taking over Nihiwatu with James McBride and continuing to develop it under the name Nihi Sumba. I wanted to show them the importance of preserving places like this, with their culture and their traditions. And it worked. Today, all three of my sons are involved in the Burch Family Foundation, supporting local initiatives across Sumba.

Q: *Nihi Sumba is often described as a luxury resort with a soul. How do you combine exclusive comfort with responsibility toward the local community?*
A: We don't want to be just one more anonymous luxury resort. We want to be a place that touches people, a place that makes a difference. I believe responsible luxury means offering beauty and comfort while giving something back to the environment and the community. Nihi lies at the edge of the wilderness, surrounded by powerful, untamed nature. And our guests feel it when they experience the horses galloping along the beach, the stillness of the rice paddies, the warmth of the local people. We want them to be aware that their stay helps support the island and its community.

"Our guests know that their stay helps support the island and its community."

Q: *A key focus of your commitment lies in education, especially for children. Why is this so important to you?*
A: Because education is where it all starts. When we give children opportunities, we are not only changing their lives, but we are also changing the future of the entire island. We build schools, support teachers, provide school supplies, and make sure every child receives a hot meal every day. The English lessons we introduced open doors for them, not only in tourism but also in how they think. I believe in these children. And I believe that they can achieve great things if we give them the chance.

Q: *How can your guests be part of this vision?*
A: By coming here with their eyes and hearts open. Many join us on school visits, help distribute meals, or play with the children. These encounters have meaning. They change people by creating connections. I cover all administrative costs of the foundation myself, so that every donation goes directly where it is needed. Many of our guests remain connected long after they have returned

"True luxury means preserving the island's unique nature and culture."

home, and some even come back to pitch in themselves. That makes me proud.

Q: *You also support healthcare and clean water initiatives. What impact has this commitment had so far?*
A: We opened health clinics on Sumba where hundreds of thousands of people have already received medical care. One of the things that moved me most was our success in fighting malaria. In some regions, infection rates have dropped by over 90%. We have also achieved a great deal when it comes to the drinking water supply. Today, more than 30,000 people have access to clean water. And every day we see what that means in concrete terms—when a child grows up healthy, when a mother breathes a sigh of relief. For me, that is true luxury: knowing that a project like this can change lives.

"Our guests visit villages, experience festivities, see how people weave, cook, worship, and celebrate."

Q: *Sumba has a rich culture. How important is it to you that your guests not only see it but truly understand it?*
A: It is deeply important to me. We don't just build in the traditional style with its high roofs and open structures; we live the culture. Almost all our staff come from the region. Our guests visit villages, experience festivities, see how people weave, cook, worship, and celebrate. I myself take part in the traditional Pasola ritual every year. For me, culture is not an accessory, it is the heartbeat of this place. Those who visit Sumba should not just spend their time relaxing, they should understand how rich this island is and how much we can learn from it.

Q: *Looking to the future, what is your vision for responsible luxury?*
A: I hope that travel becomes more conscious. That luxury no longer means isolating yourself, but connecting with people and their culture. At Nihi Sumba, we think far beyond the resort. True luxury today means preserving the island's unique nature, culture, and Marapu religion while sustainably supporting local development. When a guest leaves saying, "What I experienced here touched me, it changed me and how I think," then I know we are on the right path. That is my vision for Nihi Sumba.

Chris Burch: "I believe in these children. And I believe that they can achieve great things if we give them the chance."

NIHI SUMBA

Finding Bliss in the Breaking Waves

LUXURY WITHOUT A DRESS CODE, WILD NATURE WITH NATIVE SUMBA HORSES, THE UNTAMED FREEDOM OF SURFING THE INDIAN OCEAN—NIHI SUMBA IS A DREAMLIKE CORNER OF THE WORLD WHERE INSPIRING ENCOUNTERS TOUCH YOUR HEART FOREVER.

Opposite page: The bay off Nihi Sumba is one of the most beautiful spots for surfing in all of Asia.

Above: As you take a refreshing dip in your own pool, your gaze wanders through lush gardens out into the vast Indian Ocean.

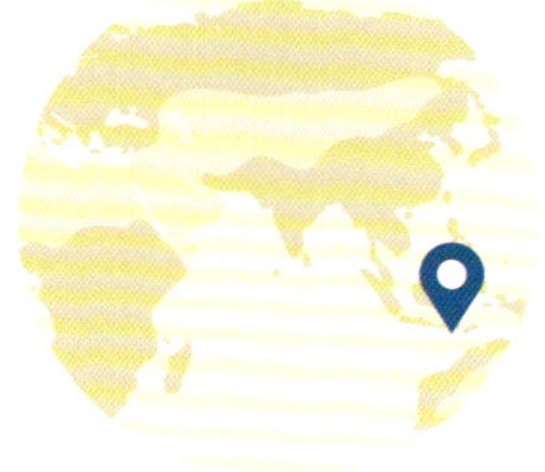

Where: On the western part of the Indonesian island of Sumba, between terraced rice paddies and sandy beaches

What: 28 individually designed villas with private pools and ocean views
Vibe: Casual, in touch with nature and local culture

Above: Gazing at the magnificent Sumba horses from the pool is a once-in-a-lifetime experience!

Opposite page, left: Surfing lessons for kids and teenagers on the seemingly endless Nihiwatu Beach.

Opposite page, right: The Spa Safari offers three routes to the hotel's spa: on foot, horseback, or by safari vehicle.

Nihi Sumba achieves something quite unusual for luxury resorts. Not only do you stay among the breathtaking scenic beauty of this Indonesian island world, but you also get to experience genuine connections with the country's culture, ancient traditions, and local community. The location alone is remarkable. The private villas are nestled between nearly pristine beach sands and the lush green of the jungle vegetation and terraced rice paddies. The accommodations combine Sumbanese architecture with luxury in a tropical, laid-back style. Choose between a spectacular treehouse above the bay or a seaside garden villa, both offering breathtaking views of the Indian Ocean. Each villa tells its own unique story and invites you to unwind by your spacious private pool.

Down at the beach you will find not only beautiful, fine sand, but also the legendary surf and its famous 'Perfect Left' wave, making Nihi Sumba a paradise for surfers. Surfing lessons are a must here, including for children, and anyone who rides their first wave after a short lesson will cherish that moment forever. Watching the famous Sumba horses gallop through the bay is another spectacular sight, making Nihi Sumba the perfect place for your first ride. The resort works closely with the Sumba Foundation, which supports local inhabitants with programs focused on education, health, and sustainable economic development. As a guest, you can visit health clinics and schools to see these initiatives firsthand and connect with local people in the process.

SWIMMING WITH HORSES

The diverse adventure program for the whole family includes horseback riding on the beach, swimming with the water-loving Sumba horses, hiking through the wilderness, and cooking and weaving workshops that immerse you in the rich local culture. The children's program is also designed to embrace this authentic, wild island atmosphere. For parents, the extraordinary Spa Safari features a holistic blend of wilderness and wellness. The resort restaurants also offer moments of indulgence with light local cuisine and Japanese specialties of the highest caliber.

HIGHLIGHTS FOR KIDS & TEENS:

- Surfing lessons and swimming with horses on one of Indonesia's most beautiful beaches
- Creative workshops to learn about the island's traditional craftsmanship
- Children's program with nature experiences and plenty of exercise
- Sports programs for children, from horseback riding to yoga
- Making friends with local children while playing beach games and taking English lessons

ACTIVITIES OFFERED AT THE RESORT:

- Activities on the beach: horseback riding, surfing, snorkeling, and swimming with horses
- Spa treatments, yoga, and meditation with a view of the Indian Ocean
- Visit Sumba Foundation projects to actively experience local culture and engagement
- Family picnics at the waterfall, private cocktails at sunset, and dinners on the beach

WHY WE LOVE IT—OUR FAMILY EXPERIENCE:

Nihi Sumba is one of the most important places in the world for us. Wild, beautiful, and deeply rooted in local traditions, this sanctuary of well-being never ceases to move us. The nature around the resort is untamed and pristine, and there are opportunities everywhere to immerse yourself in the island life. When visiting the Sumba Foundation's projects, we had the opportunity to join in the school lessons and visit the clinic to see how they successfully combat malaria. Our children played on the beach with local boys. Some of the children even came to take a swim with their water buffaloes. It was such an extraordinary moment that we still reminisce about it today. Nihi Sumba was also the place where we discovered new sides to ourselves. Our youngest was so proud when he surfed his first wave! Our eldest discovered his love for yoga and Pilates and, like all of us at Nihi Sumba, was suddenly completely at one with himself, so relaxed in one of the most beautiful yoga pavilions, with a view of the roaring ocean and the Sumba horses prancing by. For us, Nihi Sumba has long been more than just a vacation destination—it is a place close to our hearts, one we return to again and again.

BAWAH RESERVE

Far from Home, Surrounded by Nature

SUMPTUOUSLY ELEGANT TENTED SUITES AMID A PRISTINE NATURAL LANDSCAPE, WITH A SUSTAINABLE CONCEPT DESIGNED TO PRESERVE THIS PARADISE: AN ISLAND ADVENTURE IN HARMONY WITH THE RHYTHM OF THE OCEAN.

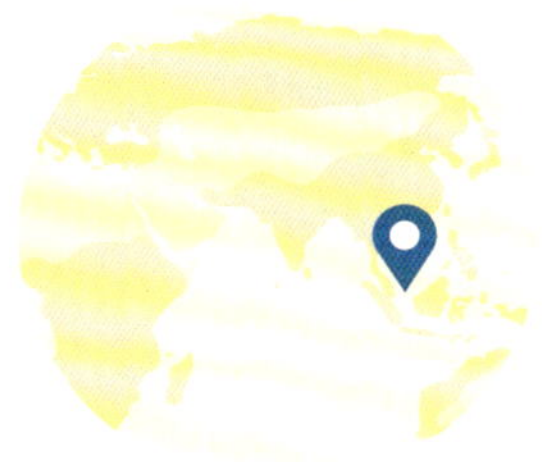

Where: Indonesia's remote Anambas archipelago between Borneo and Malaysia, northeast of Singapore

What: 36 accommodations including tented suites, bungalows, treehouse lodge suites, and villas
Vibe: Relaxed boho chic in an exclusive paradise

Leaving everyday life completely behind comes easily at the pristine nature paradise of Bawah Reserve. These six remote islands in Indonesia's Anambas archipelago in the South China Sea can only be reached by seaplane. The adventure begins the moment you arrive, for adults and children alike.
The accommodations are extraordinary: upscale private villas designed as tented suites, bungalows over the water, and tree houses, each offering generous space for pure relaxation. The villas on land are nestled between the lush jungle greenery and the beach. Throughout the resort, you can sense a deep respect for nature and a commitment to protecting this priceless ecosystem. The villas were built using the island's own natural materials, applying sustainable practices with comprehensive water treatment systems, zero-waste principles, and solar-generated electricity. As a guest, you are invited to actively participate in conservation efforts protecting coral reefs and sea turtles, creating unforgettable experiences for the entire family.

AN ISLAND-WIDE PLAYGROUND FOR ADVENTURE

A private island realm featuring three crystal-clear lagoons, a dozen porcelain-white beaches, and nothing but blue ocean stretching to every horizon, Bawah Reserve has evolved from an insider secret among trendsetters to a relaxed haven for parents and children. Traditional children's entertainment is unnecessary here, and that is precisely what makes it so appealing to children and teenagers: The entire island's pristine wilderness becomes one vast playground for adventure and discovery.

You'll find snorkeling and sailing in lagoons, open-air movies and campfires on the beach, and family picnics in hidden coves. Visitors of all ages are sure to make memories. Choose your own pace of adventure from a multitude of activities: water sports ranging from stand-up paddleboarding to snorkeling, land-based activities like croquet and tennis, an exploration of local cuisine, or a lesson on the ancient Indonesian art of batik. You can also simply surrender yourself to the spa, where the daily pampering is as integral to the island experience as the exceptional dining at the four restaurants and bars between the treetops and the beach.

Previous page: Vacation in an unspoiled island paradise: Bawah Reserve exists in perfect harmony with nature.

Left page: Watching the sunset from villas overlooking the lagoon is an experience that never grows old.

This page: From family-friendly nature hikes to kayaking excursions through the lagoon, endless discoveries await all around this island paradise.

HIGHLIGHTS FOR KIDS & TEENS:

- Diving, snorkeling, stand-up paddleboarding, kayaking, sailing & more in the lagoons
- Experience sustainability first-hand as part of environmental projects like reef protection and recycling
- Private beach picnics like Robinson Crusoe
- Bonfire evenings on the beach and family movies under the stars

ACTIVITIES OFFERED AT THE RESORT:

- Daily spa treatment included
- Yoga and Pilates in the heart of nature with experienced instructors
- Guided hikes, stargazing, and island safaris
- Dining in secluded coves and sailing at sunset
- Experience local culture: Indonesian cooking classes, batik workshops, and sustainability projects

WHY WE LOVE IT—OUR FAMILY EXPERIENCE:

Bawah Reserve radiates a magical feeling of nature: Even the casual tented style of the villas gave us the sense of being in harmony with nature. Here, luxury is defined by unique experiences: Everything became an adventure, from breakfast in a tree house to picnics on uninhabited islands and sailing at sunset. Our eldest loved participating in coral conservation projects during dives along the reef. We experienced everything here so intensively that Bawah will forever remain in our hearts.

CAPELLA UBUD

A Jungle Camp with a Fairytale Feeling

WHERE FANTASY AND REALITY CONVERGE: AT CAPELLA UBUD YOU LIVE IN JUNGLE TENTS PERCHED ON THE KELIKI VALLEY, ENJOYING VIBRANTLY COLORFUL OPULENCE—SECLUDED YET WITHIN EASY REACH OF AUTHENTIC CULTURAL EXPERIENCES.

Where: At the heart of the Indonesian island of Bali, in the vicinity of its cultural center of Ubud

What: 23 extravagant tented suites, nestled in the jungle
Vibe: Surrounded by nature and secluded, charming, and luxurious

Left: The resort's main pool shines like a jewel in the jungle.

Opposite page, top left: Balinese tradition and warm hospitality await you at Capella Ubud.

Opposite page, top right: Breakfast with a view in the soft morning light—there is no nicer way to start your day ...

Opposite page, bottom: Bright colors and the blend of Balinese and Western elements create unique and cozy lodge interiors.

HIGHLIGHTS FOR KIDS & TEENS:

- Jungle exploration with nature guides
- Creative arts and crafts and Balinese ceremonies
- Private outdoor movie nights with popcorn at your own tent
- Child-friendly menus, sustainable family workshops and cooking courses

ACTIVITIES OFFERED AT THE CAMP:

- Guided hikes through rice paddies and the jungle
- Local cultural experiences: visits to temples and villages in the vicinity
- Bike or ebike tours to Ubud and the countryside
- Yoga in the jungle pavilion, prana healing, and Balinese meditation

A profound tranquility envelops guests at Capella Ubud from the moment of arrival. Only the symphony of the jungle, punctuated by melodic birdsong, surrounds this wonderful retreat near Keliki, nestled in the heart of Bali's pristine rainforest.

The 23 luxurious tented suites, elevated on stilts and hidden under the emerald canopy of the surrounding treetops, emerge like an enchanted vision from a storybook realm. The unique, playful design by a celebrated architect is brimming with allusions to Balinese history. The resort's commitment to sustainability permeates everyday life, and it already began in the planning stage. Everything was built without felling a single tree! The suites are cocoons of serenity, while the private pools seem to hover weightlessly before each one, so seamlessly do these oases of relaxation blend into the natural landscape that surrounds them. Capella Ubud offers spa treatments in the wellness tents or the intimate sanctuary of your suite, and a swim in the large main pool transports you to a completely different, magical world.

EXPERIENCE BALINESE CUISINE AND CULTURE

Guests can savor Bali's flavorful cuisine in the resort's restaurants, during private dinners, and on jungle picnics, while cooking classes offer opportunities to learn how to cook these traditional dishes. Cultural immersion remains central to the experience, with activities designed for both children and adults: Balinese ceremonies, unique traditional dances, and the local arts and crafts Ubud is famous for all become unforgettable experiences at Capella Ubud.

Opposite page: Discover the treasures of Bali for yourself: Walk through rice paddies (far left) or enjoy chocolate delicacies from local source (left).

Right: Traditional crafts and local art lend the spa an individual touch.

WHY WE LOVE IT—OUR FAMILY EXPERIENCE:

Capella Ubud fascinated us from the very first moment. It was not just the tented village's extraordinary design, but also the indescribable jungle atmosphere, brimming with relaxed tranquility, and yet giving us the feeling of being in the midst of a fairytale adventure. Our tented suite was a true family retreat: spacious, stylish, and full of surprises, including a shower under a canopy of palm trees and our own pool. The spacious outdoor living room, open to the tropical jungle, reminded us of a tree house from classic novels—with a swing, a day bed, and a panorama that never grew boring. It was the many little moments that created lasting memories at Capella Ubud: walking through the vibrant green of the rice paddies all around us, immersing ourselves in Bali's history in old black and white films in the evening while roasting marshmallows around the campfire, swimming in the main pool in the heart of the jungle, surrounded by relaxing silence and a canopy of verdant leaves. From a culinary point of view, the exclusive Asian-inspired tasting dinner in an intimate setting remains a fond memory for us adults and our children as well.

FOUR SEASONS RESORT KOH SAMUI

Paradise with a View

STYLISH LUXURY AMID TROPICAL GREENERY, WITH A GORGEOUS BEACH AND BREATHTAKING VIEWS HIGH ABOVE THE BAY: FOUR SEASONS RESORT KOH SAMUI BRINGS TOGETHER EVERYTHING FAMILIES COULD WISH FOR ON RELAXED DAYS IN THAILAND'S DREAMLIKE ISLAND WORLD.

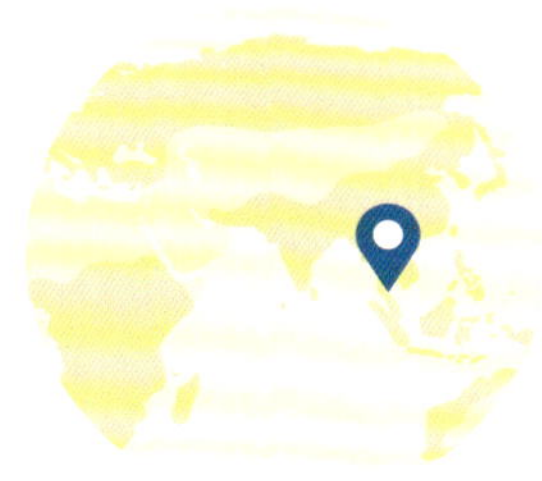

Where: On the Thai island of Koh Samui, about an hour's flight south of Bangkok

What: 70 villas and residences with private pools and sweeping views
Vibe: Sophisticated, with a feeling of tropical ease

High above the Gulf of Thailand, the villas of Four Seasons Resort Koh Samui seem to float between groves of palm trees and the dense canopy of the forest, like a scene straight out of a movie. Clean lines, premium materials, and expansive glass fronts offer breathtaking views of the water. Here, luxury feels completely natural. The architecture of these elegant hideaways harmoniously blends design and nature, from spacious decks to private pools overlooking the vast horizon. The dreamy atmosphere infuses each moment. At breakfast on the hillside terraces, your gaze drifts across the sea, shimmering in countless shades of blue, so mesmerizing you cannot help but wish time would stand still so you could savor it endlessly. The pool and spa are cradled in lush vegetation high above the bay, creating space for new perspectives, while down at the beach, the water sparkles invitingly. Across generations, every member of the family finds their own refuge to unwind at Four Seasons Resort Koh Samui. A charming beachfront children's club offers attentive childcare, inviting children to play, create, and enjoy nature-inspired activities. One special highlight for both children and adults is a training session in traditional Muay Thai in a spectacular boxing ring high in the hills.

EXPLORE STUNNING ISLAND WORLDS

There is much to discover around the resort for explorers of all ages, if you can tear yourself away from the panoramic pool and the beach. Discover a different side of Koh Samui with family kayaking and stand-up paddleboard tours along the coast, private boat trips to hidden beaches, or visits to local temples and markets. Culinary experiences at the resort are as varied as they are refined, from private barbecues at your villa and authentic Thai cuisine to cocktails at sunset on the deck and seafood on the beach, always perfectly crafted and in a magnificent setting.

Previous pages: While savoring authentic Thai cuisine and drinks on the restaurant terrace at sunset, you feel as if you are floating above the treetops.

Opposite page: Private boat trips through the almost surreal turquoise waters reveal secluded beaches.

Left: The private hillside villa pools promise endless splashing fun with breathtaking views.

Below: Experience Thailand's national sport, Muay Thai, in the spectacularly located boxing ring (left). Thoughtful design down to the finest detail defines the atmosphere of the luxuriously appointed residences (right).

HIGHLIGHTS FOR KIDS & TEENS:

- Beachfront children's club with creative activities and games
- Program for teens featuring water sports, beach games, and Muay Thai boxing classes
- Family-friendly Thai cooking classes
- Beach evenings with movies, games, and snacks
- Spa treatments designed for children

ACTIVITIES OFFERED AT THE RESORT:

- Water sports, including snorkeling, kayaking, stand-up paddleboarding, and sailing
- Culinary moments, such as private barbecues, picnics, and cocktails at sunset
- Outdoor fitness: Muay Thai high above the treetops, yoga with sea views, and a modern gym
- Nature-inspired relaxation with spa treatments in a coconut grove
- Go on diverse island adventures and explore temples, waterfalls, markets, and secluded coves

WHY WE LOVE IT—OUR FAMILY EXPERIENCE:

Our days at Four Seasons Resort Koh Samui began perfectly with a leisurely breakfast and sweeping views across the sparkling sea. The beachfront children's club was equally enchanting, full of thoughtful details. Our youngest dove straight into playtime—from face painting to beach evenings, where he roasted marshmallows by the fire, face painted like a tiger and bubbling with laughter. The sound of the waves provided a soothing backdrop while we adults enjoyed a moment to ourselves. Family vacation was redefined here in the most elegant way imaginable.

Fall in Love with an Island Paradise

TWO ISLANDS OFF CAMBODIA'S COAST WITH A HEART FOR THE LOCAL COMMUNITY: SONG SAA BLENDS SUSTAINABILITY WITH ROMANTIC, RELAXING LUXURY.

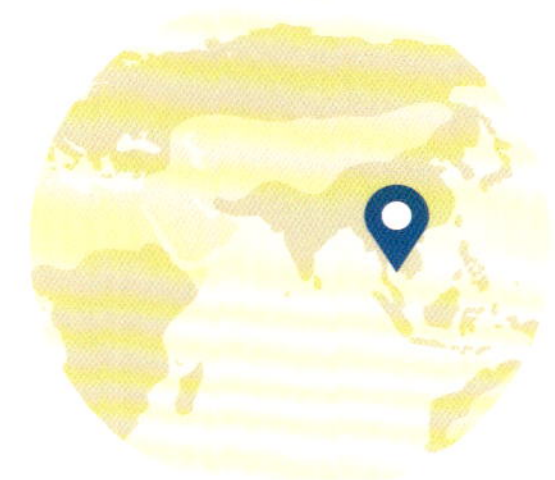

Where: On the private island duo of Song Saa in the Koh Rong archipelago off the coast of Cambodia

What: 24 sustainably built villas with private pools
Vibe: Immersed in nature, private with generous individual space

Two islands made for each other: The idyllic twin islands of Koh Ouen and Koh Bong in the Cambodian Koh Rong archipelago are home to the eco-luxury resort Song Saa Private Island. Song Saa means "the sweethearts" in Khmer, and the curving footbridge connecting the two islands symbolizes the deep bond between people and nature that is palpable throughout the resort. From day one, sustainability and local community engagement and empowerment were fundamental to the resort's design. The generously proportioned private villas on the South Island, some over water, some on land, strike a perfect balance between luxurious touches like private infinity pools and ecologically compatible architecture. Built using local materials from renewable sources, the villas feature stylish upcycled pieces crafted from driftwood by local artisans.
Song Saa implements its ecological principles for all to see: Ocean and mangrove forest conservation, along with tree planting and recycling projects, are part of the activities offered to guests of all ages. Another unique feature is the resort's own "island time." Clocks—if you need them here at all—are set forward one hour to ensure a relaxed rhythm of life from sunrise to sunset.

EXPERIENCES TO LAST A LIFETIME

The individually tailored program for children offers plenty of freedom to explore, featuring treasure hunts in the nature reserve on North Island, visits to fishing villages, snorkeling on coral reefs, and kayaking through mangrove forests. Meanwhile, parents can unwind in the spa overlooking the ocean, enjoying treatments with local healing plants and traditional meditation practices. The spirit of discovery also extends to the Cambodian cuisine; beyond the beachfront and the restaurants over the water, surprise dinners await in secret locations. And it's not just children who love these culinary adventures!

Previous page: Paradise with a sustainable touch—Song Saa is Cambodia's first luxury eco-resort on private islands.

Left: The carefully selected private villas are spacious and built with local, natural materials.

Below: You can dine in extraordinary locations with breathtaking views—why not in the middle of an infinity pool?

Opposite page: Experiencing nature on and around the island by paddling through mangrove forests and exploring the organic garden.

ACTIVITIES OFFERED AT THE RESORT:

- Spa treatments featuring local healing plants, plus yoga and meditation overlooking the ocean
- Hands-on projects about sustainability, the environment, and other educational subjects
- Cooking classes, guided herb walks, and cultural immersion in Khmer traditions
- Picnics, private dining, and sunset cocktails on secluded beaches

HIGHLIGHTS FOR KIDS & TEENS:

- Treasure hunts, nature adventures, and learning about culture in local fishing villages
- Eco-workshops on coral conservation, upcycling, and tree planting
- Snorkeling outings to discover the abundant marine life right outside your villa
- Kayak tours through mangroves and tranquil bays, stand-up paddleboarding, and boat excursions
- Endless freedom to play and explore

WHY WE LOVE IT—OUR FAMILY EXPERIENCE:

The closeness to nature and the local people on Song Saa inspired all of us. Hunting for treasures, planting trees, experiencing the resort foundation's educational projects in the villages, paddling through mangrove forests—all these experiences shaped our view of this wonderful island world! We were even served adventures for dinner: Every afternoon, we were warmly invited to mysterious locations around the island, where culinary delights featuring local ingredients were conjured up exclusively for us—just as exceptional as in the main restaurant, where you feel suspended above the ocean.

ZANNIER PHUM BAITANG

Emerald Splendor and Jungle Temples

A HAVEN OF TRANQUILITY FOR EXPLORING THE BREATHTAKING TEMPLES OF ANGKOR WAT: PHUM BAITANG IS AN OASIS IN THE HEART OF CAMBODIA, QUIETLY ENCHANTING VISITORS WITH ITS MAGIC.

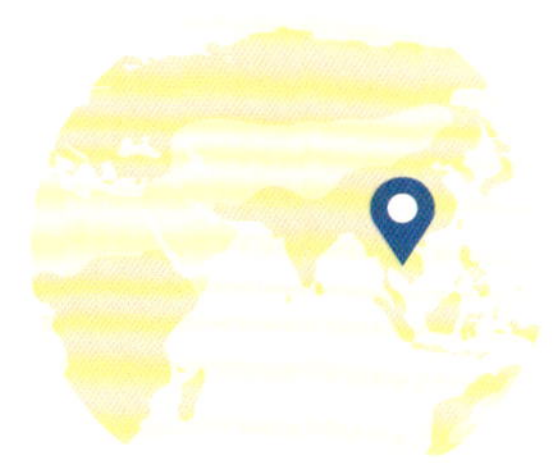

Where: Located near Siem Reap, close to Angkor Wat, the most famous temple complex in Cambodia

What: 45 stilted villas in a garden landscape reminiscent of a traditional village
Vibe: Relaxed, welcoming, and traditional

Left: The 50-meter main pool offers children plenty of space to splash around in and cool off.

Opposite page, top and bottom right: Magical evening light—the setting sun softly reflected in the smooth waters of the infinity pool.

Opposite page, bottom left: Stilted villas with understated elegance in traditional Khmer architecture.

HIGHLIGHTS FOR KIDS & TEENS:

- Discover the resort's rice paddies, gardens, and water buffaloes
- Lots of room to play in the resort's protected natural environment
- International cuisine for children: special menus and cooking workshops featuring Khmer dishes
- Experience a traditional Khmer school in the neighborhood

ACTIVITIES OFFERED AT THE RESORT:

- Guided tours, including sunrise tours, to the temples of Angkor Wat
- Bike trips in the surrounding area, visits to the market, and cooking classes with the chef
- Treatments in the spa's temple-like atmosphere
- Drinks at sunset in the historic Khmer farmhouse by the pool

On the doorstep of Cambodia's legendary Angkor Wat temple complex, one particular place has gone from sleepy roadside village to bustling tourist center: Siem Reap. It is almost surprising to discover a resort here that serves as a seemingly rustic refuge of tranquility and seclusion. Surrounded by rice paddies and sugar palms, with 45 villas in traditional stilted architecture, Zannier Phum Baitang is reminiscent of an authentic Khmer village. Built and furnished using natural materials from the surrounding area, the villas exude an understated, elegant aesthetic, offering oases for the entire family—ideal for relaxing after thrilling expeditions to the enchanted jungle temples of Angkor Wat.

"GREEN VILLAGE" WITH A SUSTAINABLE CONCEPT

Phum Baitang means "green village" in Khmer, and this proves true in more ways than one. Beyond the lush green of the rice paddies gently swaying in the breeze, the resort's award-winning master concept is also sustainably green, from ecological water management to social engagement in the local community. In the children's club program, even the youngest children can experience traditional culture, participate in the rice harvest, and discover what school is like for Cambodian children. Visits to historic temples and the floating villages of Tonlé Sap offer unforgettable experiences for the whole family, and the resort grounds provide plenty of activities as well. Cooking classes teach guests to prepare authentic Khmer dishes using rice harvested from the resort paddies, which also serve as a wonderful natural playground for children. How about a bike ride to the surrounding villages? Or a relaxing day by the magnificent infinity pool, or in the spa with its temple-like ambiance? The two restaurants with local and international cuisine also offer child-friendly menus, making them perfect for families.

Opposite page: Child-friendly supervision in the children's club and a huge outdoor area to run around in are the ideal combination for a successful vacation with children.

Above: The rice paddies in the heart of the resort are part of its sustainable planning concept.

WHY WE LOVE IT—OUR FAMILY EXPERIENCE:

Zannier Phum Baitang was our "emerald splendor" in the heart of Cambodia. With its stilted villas nestled among rice paddies, the resort resembled a traditional village—stylish, authentic, and not the least bit contrived. We loved the tranquil, natural atmosphere from the very first moment: the soft creaking of the wooden walkways underfoot, the grace of the palm trees swaying gently in the wind, the warm light of the setting sun reflected in the water. On the way to breakfast, we watched workers harvesting rice, and in the evening, we enjoyed quiet, almost meditative moments in the more than 100 years old farmhouse—the most beautiful place for us to experience the brilliant red sunsets over the rice paddies. The temples of Angkor Wat were an intense, adventurous experience, and we were all the more grateful to find a place to slow down in Phum Baitang, where we experienced the magic of Cambodia with genuine hospitality and quiet, understated beauty.

SIX SENSES NINH VAN BAY

Luxury on the Rocks

SPECTACULARLY SITUATED BETWEEN ROCK FORMATIONS, THE JUNGLE, AND A CRYSTAL-CLEAR BAY, THIS UNIQUE RETREAT AMONG VIETNAM'S IMPRESSIVE NATURAL BEAUTY OFFERS THE PERFECT BALANCE OF FREEDOM AND REFUGE.

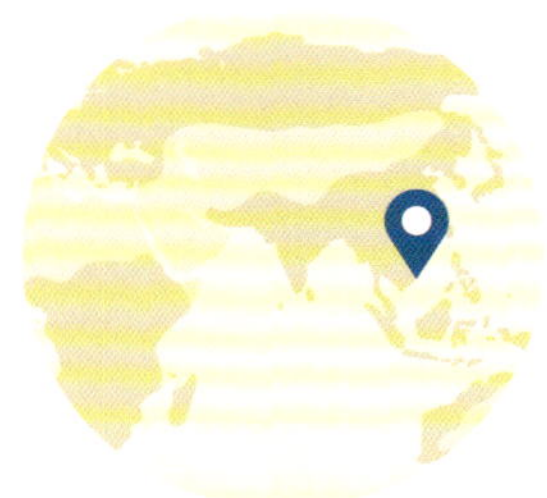

Where: On a pristine peninsula on the southeastern coast of Vietnam near Nha Trang

What: 62 villas on the beach, perched on the rocks, and above the jungle
Vibe: Secluded, offering absolute privacy

Dense jungle, dramatic granite cliffs, a wide sandy beach, and nothing on the horizon but the crystal-clear waters of the remote bay, accessible only by boat: Six Senses Ninh Van Bay on the coast of Vietnam epitomizes the "desert island" atmosphere. The 60-plus villas blend effortlessly into the pristine landscape, located on the beach and surrounded by tropical greenery, nestled into the rocks above the ocean, or perched atop the jungle canopy. Privacy is absolute, the accommodations are beyond luxurious, and every residence has its own private pool.

The airy wooden buildings reflect the resort's ecological approach with solar power, minimal waste, and an organic garden. The beach villas are particularly ideal for children, as they have direct access to the water and plenty of space to play and explore.

BOUNDLESS ADVENTURES

In Ninh Van Bay, you can spend your time however the whole family wants. You can be as active and adventurous or as relaxed as you wish with tennis, nature trekking, fishing, or water sports on, in, and under the waves, or you can unwind in the award-winning spa. The children's club offers an extensive program including creative activities, cooking courses, and nature experiences, along with yoga for kids, wellness, and playful sustainability education. Ninh Van Bay's culinary offerings focus on fresh local catches, organic vegetables from the resort's own garden, authentic Vietnamese flavors, and abundant variety. Beyond the restaurants by the pool and on the rocks with sweeping bay views, you can dine privately on the beach or in the wine cellar—or simply sail off into the sunset with canapes and drinks.

Previous page: Private residences nestled between the jungle, rock formations, and crystal-clear waters—simply breathtaking!

Arrive by boat in the bay in a relaxed state of mind, then savor fresh produce from the resort's own garden.

Below: With activities like Vietnamese cooking courses and hikes through beautiful surroundings, the resort offers diverse activities for children and teenagers.

HIGHLIGHTS FOR KIDS & TEENS:

- Children's club with a creative program, wellness for children, and cooking courses
- Experience nature: jungle adventures and hammocks over the water
- Child-friendly sustainability activities
- Open-air movies under palm trees

WHY WE LOVE IT—OUR FAMILY EXPERIENCE:

What made Ninh Van Bay so special for us was the perfect balance of seclusion and luxury, of unbridled freedom and a feeling of refuge. The world seemed far away, and yet everything we desired was there. Even arriving by boat slowed our pace down. We were surrounded by pristine nature, and the number of sustainability projects was impressive. Memorable experiences awaited all of us: a spa in the tropical jungle, Vietnamese cooking, and our boys catching their first fish and gliding through beautiful bays on water skis.

ACTIVITIES OFFERED AT THE RESORT:

- Watersports in the bay: snorkeling, diving, kayaking, and water skiing
- Yoga with ocean views and spa treatments with ingredients straight from the organic garden
- Guided hikes to hidden lookout points
- Sunset tours by boat

Spectacularly embedded in rocky outcrops, the villa complexes offer both seclusion and luxury.

SIX SENSES CON DAO

Beautiful Island Getaway

WITH GORGEOUS BEACHES AND A FOCUS ON ECOLOGY, HISTORY, AND SUSTAINABLE LIVING, CON DAO OFFERS FAMILIES A REFLECTIVE VIETNAMESE RETREAT WHERE TRANQUILITY MEETS LUXURY.

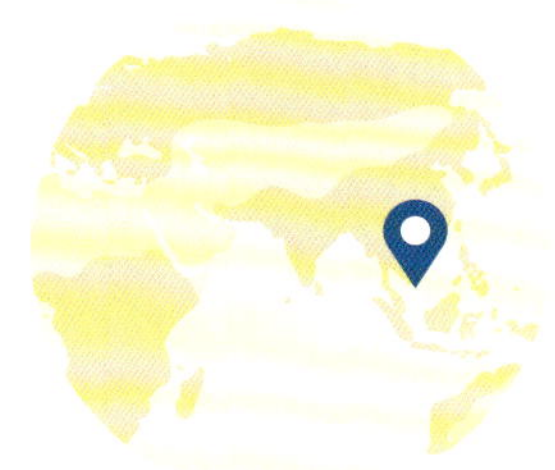

Where: On the remote island archipelago of Con Dao off the southern coast of Vietnam

What: 50 beach villas in the style of a fishing village, with private infinity pools
Vibe: Quiet and relaxed, offering privacy

This remote archipelago off the southern coast of Vietnam is truly unique. Once notorious for being a prison island, Con Dao is now a magnificent natural environment that is home to diverse flora and fauna. Here, where colorful coral reefs surround the islands and you can spot rare bird species and marine life like the exotic dugong, you will find the extraordinary resort Six Senses Con Dao. The bright, airy, wooden beach villas resemble traditional Vietnamese fishermen's houses. From your private infinity pool you have a direct view of the ocean, just a few steps away from the endless golden sandy beach. The resort preserves this beach as protected breeding grounds for sea turtles. This appreciation of nature and wildlife conservation is actively shared with guests; anyone fortunate enough to accompany newly emerged hatchlings on their first tentative journey into the ocean will recognize what a unique and protected place Con Dao is.

SUSTAINABILITY IN PRACTICE

The resort's ecological approach is visible everywhere. It is plastic-free, generates electricity with solar panels, grows fresh produce for its restaurants in organic gardens, and invests in local educational projects. Guests can experience this connection to nature in various workshops, and even the wide range of activities available at the children's club covers sustainability concepts in playful ways. Even dining takes on an adventurous character. In addition to the restaurants, private dinners await on the beach, in the wine cellar, or amid the organic gardens. Water sports are particularly spectacular in the crystal-clear waters surrounding the island, and diving among the coral reefs reveals the vibrant underwater world in all its glory. Yet despite these many activities, Con Dao provides ample opportunity for peace and relaxation. Experiencing the sounds of the ocean and the lush jungle greenery with all your senses creates a lasting connection to this beautiful island paradise.

ACTIVITIES OFFERED AT THE RESORT:

- Water sports around the island: snorkeling, diving, kayaking, and paddleboarding
- Cultural excursions: historical sites, fishing villages, and nature spotting in Con Dao National Park
- Yoga, meditation, and holistic treatments in the spa, surrounded by water lilies
- Local cooking classes with ingredients from the resort's own organic gardens
- Private dining experiences at unique locations throughout the resort

HIGHLIGHTS FOR KIDS & TEENS:

- A diverse children's club program with both physical and creative activities
- Child-friendly workshops: mask-making, T-shirt painting, pizza-making, and much more
- Extraordinary nature experiences: accompanying baby turtles on their journey, beach games, and movies in the jungle
- Environmental appreciation, community, and culture experienced through play

From observing baby turtles (above) to exploring the beach and paddleboarding through the crystal-clear waters (left), you can experience the island with all your senses.

The pristine beach of Con Dao National Park is perfect for long walks.

WHY WE LOVE IT—OUR FAMILY EXPERIENCE:

Con Dao showed us an unexpectedly calm and contemplative side of Vietnam, on this island with its many different facets and surprising experiences. We were particularly moved by the connection to the country's history. Once a place of horror, Con Dao was a prison archipelago dominated by oppression and suffering. Confronting this past is not easy, but it is well worth it and leaves you with lasting impressions. The encounters with local people were all the more touching. Their unforgettable kindness—open, sincere, and full of warmth—stands in impressive contrast to the dark past. The location of the resort alone, at the foot of verdant Elephant Mountain overlooking the blue expanse of the sea, was fascinating, almost surreal in its beauty. Our villa, stylishly designed with understated luxury, was a pleasant retreat offering abundant privacy. We had the feeling of being far from home and yet so close to what matters: the richness of nature, the calm flow of life, and encounters with wonderful people.

Above: Dinner and drinks with a view at the beachfront restaurant.

Right: Trekking up Elephant Mountain rewards hikers with spectacular views over Con Dao Bay.

Children need a home away from home

A CONVERSATION WITH LIZ BIDEN, FOUNDER OF MALEWANE, LA RESIDENCE, AND THE SILO, ABOUT FAMILY WELL-BEING RETREATS.

Q: *Mrs. Biden, what inspired you to enter the hotel business after many successful years in the fashion industry?*
A: Honestly, retirement simply is not in my nature. When I sold my fashion label at fifty, I went exactly two days before suggesting to my husband that we transform our home in the Greater Kruger Region into a hotel. I felt incredibly fortunate to have this vacation home in the African bush, filled with treasured memories—and I was compelled to share that with others through Malewane.

Q: *You often talk about the concept of "home away from home." What exactly do you mean by that?*
A: I want our guests to feel as though they are staying with friends rather than simply being a guest in a hotel room. I want to create spaces where people instantly feel at home. Any place where I spend my vacation with my family should emanate a sense of security and comfort, and this can only be achieved if it is very personal and caring, with an abundance of warmth. Whether it is at Royal Malewane or The Silo, my focus is never just about luxury for our guests, but about fostering genuine connections to the country, to the art, to the people.

Q: *You focus strongly on family-friendliness, highlighting how important it is to create spaces that work for all ages. How do you achieve this?*

"I focus on fostering authentic connections to the country, to the art, to the people."

A: Well, I love traveling for my own enjoyment, but also to create shared memories with my grandchildren, which is why I actively work to promote multi-generational travel. Nothing makes me happier than seeing children, parents, and grandparents enjoying wonderful experiences together at our properties. It is very important to me that all kinds of families feel welcome—whether they are extended families, single parents, or same-sex couples with their children.

Q: *Anyone who visits your properties immediately realizes what an important role art plays for you. Can you tell us more about that?*

"When designing each of our hotels and lodges, it is essential to me that art and children, luxury and relaxation all go hand in hand."

A: I never liked the idea of art being used exclusively for decoration in hotels. Art is so much more than that. A painting or sculpture has the power to bring a room to life. Art tells stories, creates an atmosphere of warmth. For me, even the lively interplay of intense colors is art. A perfect example is the Waterfront Lodge at Royal Malewane. In my own home, I surround myself with fantastic colors, and it makes me so happy! I had a feeling our guests would love it too. It is the unusual pieces that give a room its character, which is why I love combining old and new. For me, using existing things in a new way is as

"Art is so much more than decoration. A painting or sculpture has the power to really bring a room to life."

much an expression of creativity as it is a sign of appreciation for what a person once created.

Q: *On the one hand, art. On the other hand, children who want to let off steam. Are the two really compatible?*
A: Absolutely! When designing our hotels and lodges, it has always been important to me that art and children, luxury and informality go hand in hand. Our guests should never feel like they are walking through a museum. Comfort and a genuine feeling of well-being always come first, especially for families.

Q: *What does hosting families mean to you?*
A: Time is the most precious commodity nowadays, and people want to spend it with their family, traveling with them. Families value privacy, good service, and activities tailored to their needs. I view it as our job to offer the families who stay with us a holistic experience, to enable them to grow together while also connecting with the place and the people they encounter. It is much the same for us. We are a family business, and my son is now CEO of The Royal Portfolio, carrying forward the vision we have all built together. We consider our guests and our staff as part of this extended family—and I think everyone feels that.

Liz Biden: "As a family-run business, we strive to make each of our accommodations a home away from home, so that every stay is a distinctly personal experience."

Three Iconic Lodges and the Big Five

ROYAL MALEWANE TAKES THE SAFARI EXPERIENCE TO A NEW LEVEL. IN ONE OF SOUTH AFRICA'S MOST BEAUTIFUL GAME RESERVES, THREE EXCEPTIONAL VENUES WELCOME GUESTS WITH EXTRAVAGANT DESIGN, CURATED ART, AND FIRST-CLASS SERVICE.

Where: In the Thornybush Game Reserve, part of Kruger National Park in northeastern South Africa

What: 3 individual safari lodges, each with only a few suites
Vibe: Luxurious, elegant, warm hospitality

Kruger National Park, one of Africa's largest and most renowned game reserves, sprawls across South Africa's far north. Nestled within its heart lies the private Thornybush Game Reserve, home to three exclusive Royal Malewane properties. At the flagship Malewane Lodge, classic elegance meets quintessential safari style. The two Royal Suites are ideal for families, while the spacious Farmhouse of Farmstead Lodge, with its own terrace and pool, offers both privacy and room for children to enjoy; its playful vintage charm creating a true home away from home. The vibrant, imaginatively designed suites at Waterside Lodge provide equally welcoming spaces, perfect for unforgettable family stays. Dining at Malewane Lodge is a feast for the senses. Innovative menus tailored to personal preferences are served in elegant dining salons overlooking waterholes where elephants and other wildlife gather. Should you desire in-villa pampering, dedicated butler teams ensure every detail is taken care of. For a touch of adventure, nothing compares to a bush dinner by lantern light under starry skies, with crackling campfires adding to the romance.

ON THE TRAIL OF THE BIG FIVE

Exclusive game drives with private vehicles, guides, and trackers offer intimate Big Five encounters—elephant, lion, rhino, leopard, and buffalo in their natural habitat. Walking safaris provide equally enriching family experiences, as expert trackers reveal smaller bush wonders through intuitive knowledge and keen observation. Learning to read animal tracks and signs captivates children and adults alike!

HIGHLIGHTS FOR KIDS & TEENS:

- Child-friendly game drives in your own safari vehicle
- Dedicated guide and tracker upon request, for safari experiences at your own pace
- Private family villas with pool, kitchen, and friendly service team
- Child-friendly cooking and creative activities
- Spa treatments for teens as well

ACTIVITIES OFFERED AT THE RESORT:

- Game drives by day and night, accompanied by world-class guides and trackers
- A nature experience in a class of its own: bush walks for all ages
- Relax with spa treatments, fitness activities, and in the pool
- Gourmet cuisine, also enjoyed al fresco

Left: Wildlife experiences (almost) within arm's reach—elephants visiting the private pool, tracking with first-class trackers.

Above: In a private jeep with expert guides, the safari experience is tailored to the family's desires.

With its expansive pool directly beside the dam, Waterside Lodge truly lives up to its name.

WHY WE LOVE IT—OUR FAMILY EXPERIENCE:

Royal Malewane's three camps—the founder's former home at Malewane Lodge, along with Farmstead Lodge and Waterside Lodge—are all as expressive as they are different. Each manages to blend seamlessly into the surrounding bush landscape in its own way. We were especially taken with the colorful, vibrant style of Waterside Lodge—bright colors, bold yet elegantly composed and in perfect harmony with nature. What touched us most across all the lodges, however, was the exceptional warmth of the entire team—genuine, warm, and a real joy to meet. At Royal Malewane, they made us feel less like hotel guests and more like friends coming to visit. Although we stayed at several lodges, "our" own small team accompanied us throughout, ensuring we felt at home from the very first moment. The wildlife encounters in Thornybush Game Reserve were just as remarkable. Sightings of the legendary Big Five are almost assured here, and we were also fortunate to spot cheetahs, African wild dogs, and a variety of birdlife. With its large pool right next to the dam, Waterside Lodge is certainly true to its name.

Above: Elegant dining deep in the bush, complete with magical flickering candlelight.

Right: Closeness to nature paired with luxurious accommodations—at Royal Malewane, these go together perfectly.

LA RESIDENCE

Wine, Expansive Views, and Colorful Design

IN FRANSCHHOEK, SOUTH AFRICA'S GOURMET MECCA, LA RESIDENCE IS A MINOR SENSATION: WINE TASTING, CULINARY HIGHLIGHTS, AND ART FOR CONNOISSEURS COUPLED WITH EXTRAORDINARY EXPERIENCES FOR YOUNGER GUESTS AS WELL.

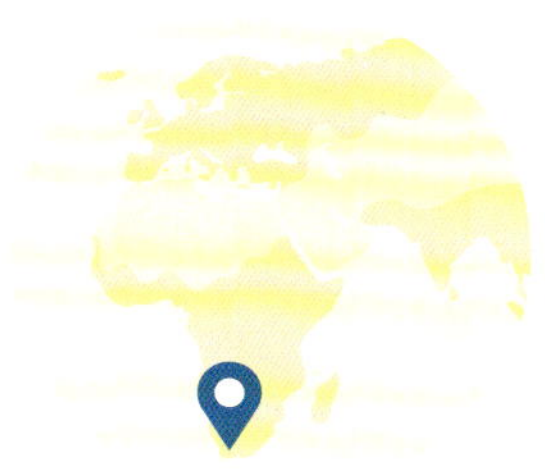

Where: In Franschhoek, South Africa's wine and gourmet center in the mountainous Western Cape province

What: 11 suites, 5 vineyard family suites and a villa with 5 bedrooms
Vibe: Opulent elegance, exceptionally personal service

Breathtakingly rugged mountains frame a wide valley with a mild climate and gentle green slopes, somewhat reminiscent of the French Alpine foothills. It is little wonder that in the 17th century a group of Huguenots settled here, feeling right at home in the Stellenbosch region! The history of Franschhoek, one of South Africa's oldest towns, begins with these settlers. Today, the probably most idyllic wine-growing region in South Africa is a destination for gourmets and art lovers.

The extravagant boutique hotel La Residence skillfully blends opposites. On the one hand, it offers a haven of serenity with a warm, family atmosphere; on the other, the culinary and cultural highlights of Franschhoek's lively gourmet scene are just a stone's throw away. The memorable, extravagant mix of design, art, and opulent elegance has a surprisingly relaxed atmosphere, even for families with children. Fine antiques, curated works of art, plush velvet, open fireplaces, and private pools characterize the spacious suites and villas designed for family stays. La Residence offers a full range of culinary delights, from gourmet breakfasts and lunches with a view to elegant afternoon teas and exquisite dinners. Beyond the hotel, the village itself tempts with a wealth of gourmet restaurants in the village vying for visitors' favor.

CYCLING, HIKING & FAMILY FUN

The beauty of the surrounding countryside invites exploration, whether on a bicycle ride or a hike through the vineyards. Picnics among the vines are just as exciting as horseback rides or a visit to the charming Old Timer Museum. True to its reputation as South Africa's epicenter of indulgence, Franschhoek also caters imaginatively to families. Many wineries offer special treats for children, such as ice cream or chocolate tastings alongside wine for adults. More than one parent might be a little envious of these delightful experiences.

Above: Nestled in picturesque vineyards and idyllic gardens, La Residence offers a panorama that you can hardly get enough of.

Right: The spacious family villa Franschhoek House offers the most exclusive service, even with a private chef.

Above left and right: The spacious family villa Franschhoek House offers a wonderful pool with sweeping views and an extravagant yet cozy interior.

Left: Guests enjoy warm colors, plenty of light, and fantastic views in the spacious lounge.

HIGHLIGHTS FOR KIDS & TEENS:

- Family villas with their own pools, kitchens, and large gardens
- Visits to animal farms, chocolate factories, and markets
- Outdoor activities for all ages: bike tours, vineyard picnics, and outings in the vicinity
- Special children's experiences at local wineries include ice cream and chocolate tasting

ACTIVITIES OFFERED AT THE RESORT:

- Wine tastings and gourmet dining experiences in the region
- Gallery visits, farm tours, and historic walking tours through Franschhoek
- Spa treatments with vineyard views
- Relaxed and active: yoga, swimming, hiking, riding

A retreat against a magnificent backdrop: La Residence unfolds like a lush oasis in the beautiful Franschhoek Valley.

WHY WE LOVE IT—OUR FAMILY EXPERIENCE:

We are devoted Franschhoek fans, and there are plenty of reasons why: an inspiring gourmet world, lush green landscapes against a breathtaking mountain backdrop, diverse activities, and above all, the very special feeling this region always gives us. We were looking for a place here where we could feel at home, and that is exactly what we found at La Residence: colorful, personal, full of warmth, a true home away from home! The entire team was thoroughly professional while greeting us all with a genuine warmth that immediately made us feel welcome. We enjoyed the special atmosphere so much, and it became a cherished ritual of ours to greet each day on the veranda looking at that incredible mountain view, a perfectly foamed latte in hand. Franschhoek offers diverse outings for the whole family. Our boys were fascinated by the Motor Museum, we explored the vineyards on horseback, visited farm animals, and were delighted to find that many wineries included children in the experience by offering ice cream or chocolate tastings.

THE SILO

Above the Rooftops of Cape Town

THE ICONIC HOTEL ON CAPE TOWN'S WATERFRONT IS A WALKABLE WORK OF ART AND ARCHITECTURAL GEM, OFFERING THE BEST VACATION VIEWS, A SPECTACULAR ROOFTOP POOL, AND GLAMOROUS CITY SUITES.

Opposite page: The Silo Rooftop offers the perfect spot for evening drinks above the twinkling lights of Cape Town.

Above: Cool off in the rooftoɔ pool with magnificent views of Lion's Head.

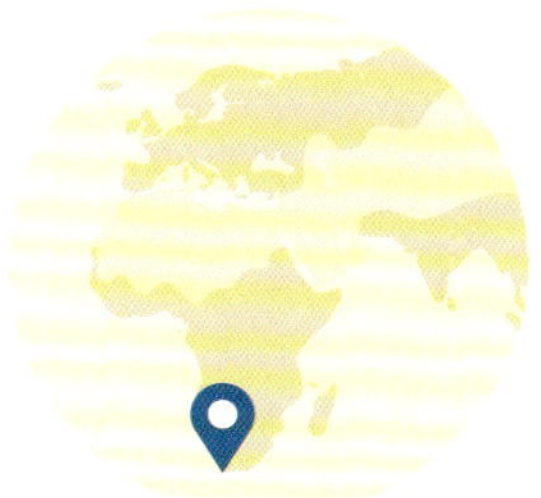

Where: In a spectacular design complex on the Victoria & Alfred Waterfront in Cape Town

What: Around 30 individually appointed suites
Vibe: Urban, iconic, bold design

The luxury version of "room with a view"—the cushion-shaped windows of the tastefully furnished suites gleam like polished diamonds.

Opposite page, left and right: Hike the trails of Kirstenbosch National Botanical Garden. The Silo's lobby also houses an impressive collection of contemporary African art.

It certainly takes ingenuity, and perhaps a spark of madness, to transform South Africa's largest grain silo into one of the country's most extraordinary hotels. The uniquely designed Silo rises above the Zeitz MOCAA, short for Zeitz Museum of Contemporary Art Africa; its striking diamond-shaped panoramic windows bringing an elegant lightness to the former concrete complex. These faceted glass structures frame what is likely the most spectacular view in Cape Town, sweeping from the ocean to Table Mountain, with breathtaking sunrises and dreamy evening light. The individually designed suites, some extending over two floors, exude an atmosphere of well-being for families. Here, too, guests enjoy their stay amid a carefully curated collection of works from the African art scene.

ART, CULTURE AND FANTASTIC VIEWS

Art is a defining element of The Silo. A dedicated art concierge offers exclusive guided tours of the Zeitz MOCAA, offering new perspectives of contemporary African creativity. The hotel is also an ideal base for exploring the Mother City: A stroll along the waterfront, a day at the beach in Camps Bay, a tour of Table Mountain—everything is within easy reach. The penguin colony on Boulders Beach and the Cape of Good Hope are also just a short drive away. Culinary pleasures abound both within The Silo and in the vibrant Waterfront district. If you still crave exercise after an enjoyable day, we recommend a somewhat strenuous but all the more rewarding tour up Lion's Head. The view from Cape Town's second "local mountain" at sunset is unsurpassed!

ACTIVITIES OFFERED AT THE RESORT:

- Visit the Zeitz MOCAA right in the building, with a personal art concierge upon request
- Explore the Waterfront district with its shops and restaurants
- Enjoy a relaxing day on the beach at Camps Bay or Clifton
- Take a sunset hike up Lion's Head

HIGHLIGHTS FOR KIDS & TEENS:

- Rooftop pool with spectacular views
- Family-friendly duplex suites with plenty of space and stunning panoramic views
- Boat trips and child-friendly museum tours
- Creative workshops and city tours tailored for children
- Outings to the Cape of Good Hope and the penguins at Boulders Beach

WHY WE LOVE IT—OUR FAMILY EXPERIENCE:

The Silo is spectacular, yet it always feels deeply personal. We have come to know this magnificent hotel in our beloved Cape Town as a place for all the senses. Just like the Mother City represents an attitude toward life for us, an artistic masterpiece between the ocean and Table Mountain, The Silo equally inspired and moved us—becoming yet another reason we will happily return here again and again. Set directly above the Zeitz MOCAA, the hotel feels like a walkable art installation: playful, bold, and extraordinary. The art concierge who guided us through the museum opened up new perspectives and ways of thinking for all of us. Thanks to its perfect location, The Silo offered us a wealth of possibilities: a city bus tour in the morning, strolling through the Waterfront district at midday, spending the afternoon at Camps Bay beach, visiting the penguins at Boulders Beach, or taking a quick trip to the Cape of Good Hope. In the evenings we could hardly decide: The sunset from Lion's Head was just as sensational as enjoying the delicious drinks and snacks in the rooftop bar, as the city lights began twinkling all around us.

The Magic of the South African Desert

TSWALU IS THE LARGEST PRIVATE GAME RESERVE IN THE COUNTRY: THREE EXCLUSIVE CAMPS, EACH DESIGNED FOR JUST A HANDFUL OF GUESTS, PROVIDE THE PERFECT BASE FOR DISCOVERING THE BREATHTAKING BEAUTY OF THE LANDSCAPE AND THE UNIQUE WILDLIFE OF THE GREEN KALAHARI.

Where: In the Northern Cape province near the border with Botswana, almost 250 miles northwest of Kimberley, the regional capital

What: 3 luxury safari camps, each positioned to take in the reserve's landscapes
Vibe: At one with nature, while sparing no elegance

Left and opposite page, top right: If luck and timing align, you may be rewarded with a truly special encounter; perhaps a cheetah, or even the rare sight of a pangolin.

Opposite page: On the move with a private 4 x 4 vehicle and guide for a unique family experience (top left). Loapi, which means "the space below the clouds" in Setswana, is a stylish tented residence with ample luxury and its own kitchen and butler staff (bottom).

HIGHLIGHTS FOR KIDS & TEENS:

- Safaris in your private vehicle with a dedicated guide, completely flexible, thoughtfully designed for families
- Horseback riding through the desert landscape (suitable for children who are experienced riders)
- Learning alongside expert rangers: tracking wildlife, observing animals, reading the night sky
- Joining and observing meerkats is a magical experience that captivates children and adults alike

ACTIVITIES OFFERED AT THE RESORT:

- Go on game drives, hikes, safaris on horseback, photography expeditions across the expansive private reserve
- Sleep out on the dunes while stargazing under the brilliant skies of the southern hemisphere
- Visit and explore research stations and conservation projects in the reserve
- Experience fine dining as an adventure with an exceptional culinary experience in the gourmet desert restaurant

Out and about with a private guide, offering both children and adults a deeper understanding of flora and fauna.

The Tswalu Kalahari Reserve stretches over more than 460 square miles, with three safari camps right in the heart of it all. For families seeking to experience the wild nature of South Africa, few experiences rival the exclusivity of the two camps, Motse and Loapi, and the private homestead Tarkuni. Set within a seemingly endless landscape where savanna transitions into desert, you can sense a special energy surrounding the exquisite suites, where acacia groves weave between gently undulating dunes and dramatic rock formations that take on an almost ethereal crimson glow in the evening sun.

THREE LUXURIOUS, DISTINCTIVE SUITES

Three of the just nine suites in Motse, designed with stylish textiles and rich natural wood, provide spacious family sanctuaries where every comfort has been carefully considered. You can enjoy magnificent sunsets from the pools at the inviting main house, overlooking the water hole where many animals gather. In Loapi's six tented safari pavilions, contemporary design embraces the essence of luxury. Here you live the dream of complete solitude within the breathtaking nature of the Kalahari, far from civilization, attended by your personal chef and dedicated butler service. The Tarkuni private villa is another microcosm combining ultimate comfort with authenticity. A culinary masterpiece awaits in the subterranean savanna restaurant, where a heritage-inspired dining experience creates culinary adventures in the heart of pristine remoteness.

All three camps share an intimate bond with the animal world, where giraffes, antelopes, buffaloes, cheetahs, and lions roam alongside increasingly rare treasures—aardvarks, pangolins, and black rhinos—offering wildlife encounters unmatched anywhere in South Africa. Families can discover the diversity and beauty of the wildlife at their own pace on private safaris with a private vehicle and guide, while learning all about the Tswalu Foundation's mission to preserve this extraordinary wilderness legacy.

Above: A refreshing dip in the pool after the photography safari—the Tarkuni private camp ensures maximum luxury.

Right: In Motse, the largest camp, you stay in elegant suites made of wood and natural stone, where every comfort has been thoughtfully anticipated.

WHY WE LOVE IT—OUR FAMILY EXPERIENCE:

The deep red earth, the gently undulating dunes, the interplay of light and shadow across the rocks—the breathtaking landscape of the Kalahari alone made Tswalu an indescribably impressive place for us. There was an abundance of wildlife to discover around our camp: oryx, giraffes, kudus, ostriches, baboons, and then suddenly we saw a cheetah in the sand! Our private safari experiences, perfectly choreographed to our family's rhythm by our dedicated guide, surpassed nearly every adventure we have ever had. We observed meerkats up close for the very first time—the sheer delight of encountering these adorable creatures is difficult to put into words! We went on desert horseback rides guided by our seasoned ranger, feeling completely secure and protected. Perhaps the most magical moment was our night in a simple but comfortable tent atop a sand dune: Just us, the sky full of twinkling stars, and the infinite expanse of the Kalahari stretching endlessly before us—a sublime moment we will never forget!!

MARATABA

Between River and Rock Formations

THIS LODGE IS PERFECT FOR ANYONE SEEKING A SPECTACULAR FAMILY SAFARI AMID STUNNING MOUNTAIN SCENERY. ALONGSIDE CLASSIC GAME DRIVES BY JEEP, BOAT TOURS ON THE RIVER REVEAL FRESH PERSPECTIVES OF SOUTH AFRICAN FLORA AND FAUNA.

Opposite page: An evening barbecue at sunset in the magical atmosphere of the lodge's gardens.

Above: The cozy tented suites combine modern comforts with proximity to nature.

Right: The large pool is the best place to cool off after an outing for children and adults alike.

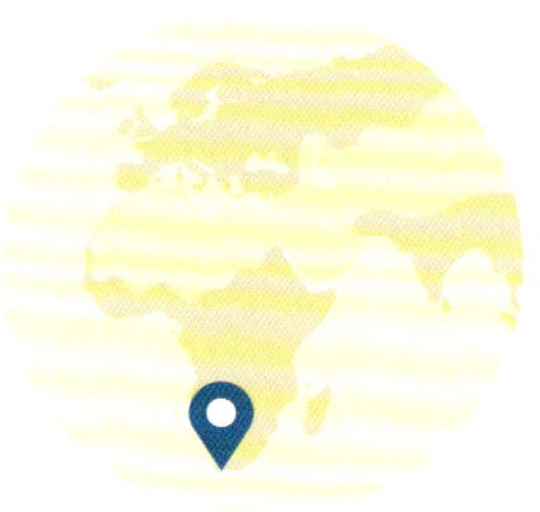

Where: Around 185 miles north of Johannesburg, near Marakele National Park

What: 15 luxurious tented suites
Vibe: family-friendly and in touch with nature, exclusive service

A photography safari set against a breathtaking panorama—as you look out over the vast plain toward the Waterberg, you are sure to spot wild animals.

High in the Waterberg massif, at the heart of the biosphere reserve in South Africa's Limpopo province, the Matlabas River rises from its source and winds through the dreamlike landscape of Marakele National Park. Nestled in a bend of the river lies the camp of Marataba private reserve, set before a panorama that feels like a painting: dramatic rock faces that seem to glow in the evening light, a fascinating mosaic of river and bush in the wide plain alive with biodiversity. Here, the landscape is not just a backdrop but the star of the show, with a wealth of experiences to match: classic game drives in open jeeps, guided bush walks with expert trackers, and countless adventures tailored to children. One special highlight is the safari by boat, which shows the richness of nature from a completely different perspective, offering the opportunity to see elephants, rhinos, giraffes, and lions, along with a dazzling variety of birds from the water.

SAFARI ADVENTURES ESPECIALLY FOR CHILDREN

At Marataba Lodge, a dedicated team of rangers and childcare specialists creates programs for the children's club designed for young explorers. On their big safari adventure, children learn to pitch camp, read tracks, and track animals, before ending the day with movies under the stars—unforgettable impressions sure to stay with them for years to come.

Life in the lodge also creates the feeling of being on an expedition. Guests stay in tented suites, stylishly furnished and offering plenty of comfort. In the family suites, children even have their very own personal retreat with a bathroom just for them. Spa treatments can be enjoyed in the privacy of the suite, while open-air dinners by the fire bowl in the lodge's gardens create magical evenings surrounded by nature. Between safaris, the pool offers the perfect spot to cool off, splash, and relax.

Below: From sustainable drinking bottles to binoculars, everything you need is provided for your family safari (left). Knowledgeable guides turn game drives into great adventures for children as well (right).

ACTIVITIES OFFERED AT THE RESORT:

- Impressive game drives, day and night
- Boat safaris along the Matlabas River
- Guided bush walks with expert guides
- Personalized experiences such as stargazing and outdoor picnics
- Workshops on nature studies and wildlife photography

HIGHLIGHTS FOR KIDS & TEENS:

- Special safaris designed for children with age-appropriate nature programs
- Bush adventures: treasure hunts and tracking with a ranger
- Stories from the wild around the evening campfire
- River safaris by boat

WHY WE LOVE IT—OUR FAMILY EXPERIENCE:

We were overwhelmed by the scenery at Marataba: the towering Waterberg rocks glowing copper in the evening sun, the golden light casting a quiet magic over everything, and ever-changing contrasts of rock, river, and wilderness. It is hard to imagine more spectacular scenery. The variety of safari experiences thrilled us as well. Exploring the reserve's wealth of wildlife not only in the classic open jeep but also by boat opened up completely new perspectives for us, and we felt very close to the animals. Our guide was warm and knowledgeable, and seeing him brimming with passion for his homeland at each wildlife sighting made our experience even more special. The wonderful lodge itself charmed us with its understated luxury, stylish atmosphere, and genuine warmth. For us, Marataba means nature, closeness, and diversity—and remains one of our very favorite safari destinations in South Africa.

BABYLONSTOREN

Country Living, African Style

A CHARMING WINERY, MAGNIFICENT GARDENS, AND FRIENDLY FARM ANIMALS FROM DONKEYS TO DUCKS: BABYLONSTOREN IS A LUXURIOUS INTERPRETATION OF LIFE ON THE FARM.

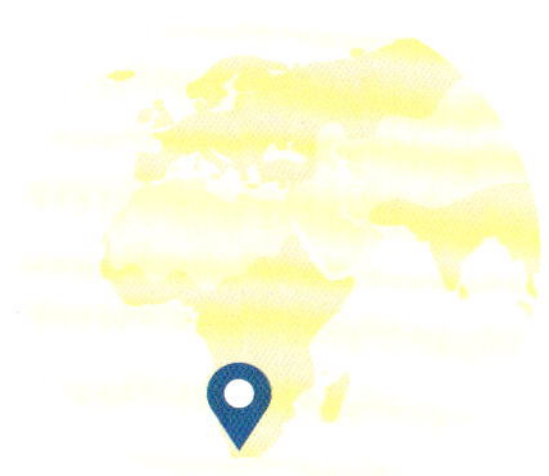

Where: In South Africa's wine region, between Stellenbosch and Paarl, an hour east of Cape Town

What: Farm hotel with suites and cottages
Vibe: In touch with nature, relaxed, plenty of open spaces

If there is one place in South Africa's Drakenstein Valley wine region that takes the "farm-to-fork" philosophy literally, it is Babylonstoren. The historic winery dating back to 1692 has evolved into a high-end hotel where country living takes on a whole new dimension. Everything produced on the roughly 500 acres of vineyards, orchards, fields, and olive groves finds its way onto the menus of the three outstanding restaurants. The kitchen gardens, where more than 300 plant species are grown, are beautifully laid out in the style of a medieval knot garden. Whether you are on a guided tour or helping with the harvest, when you stroll through them, you almost feel like you are wandering through Versailles. Families stay in charming Cape Dutch–style cottages that combine rustic charm with elegant comfort, featuring open fireplaces and private verandas overlooking the mountains.

CHILDHOOD ADVENTURES IN NATURE

Babylonstoren is much more than just a luxury hotel, it is an immersive experience for all your senses. The entire estate is a vast adventure playground for children, full of things to discover and do, such as harvesting fruits and vegetables, feeding the donkeys, gathering eggs, watching the cute ducks waddle by, crossing the pond by raft, fishing and rowing at the dam, splashing in the large pool, or enjoying a treatment in the garden spa. Each family has bicycles available for exploring the grounds.
A shuttle goes to the nearby Soetmelksvlei Farm Museum, which belongs to Babylonstoren. It is a fully working farm that operates just as it did in the 19th century, complete with fascinating live demonstrations by the blacksmith and carpenter, and more!

HIGHLIGHTS FOR KIDS & TEENS:

- Meet and feed the farm animals: donkeys, geese, chickens, turkeys, and more
- Get hands-on in the garden on guided discovery tours and fruit-picking adventures
- Go fishing at the dam followed by a picnic on the wooden jetty
- Plenty of space to play, explore, and be amazed

ACTIVITIES OFFERED AT THE HOTEL:

- Three restaurant venues featuring a "farm-to-fork" concept and themed menus
- Wine cellar, concept store, and fragrance lab
- Garden tours, bread baking, honey sampling, wine and olive oil tastings
- Wellness in the garden spa
- Canoeing, biking, hiking, and outdoor "stretch & breathe" sessions

Left: A flock of white ducks in the orchard.

Top: The whole farm is a vast natural playground with thoughtfully designed "adventure" elements.

Above: The water lily garden is part of an ingenious irrigation system.

Above: Exploring the extensive grounds is always worthwhile, on foot or on the bicycles available for the whole family.

Opposite page, top: The garden cottages are designed in the style of Cape Dutch gabled houses.

Opposite page, bottom: The spa facilities include a large indoor pool.

WHY WE LOVE IT—OUR FAMILY EXPERIENCE:

During our first stay in South Africa's wine region, we discovered Babylonstoren, a haven of well-being with an unforgettable ambiance. Its vast farm grounds are stunningly beautiful, from the sprawling orchards to the fascinating vegetable gardens reminiscent of the magnificent gardens of French palaces. Being able to help with the harvest and then sit down to a meal knowing the ingredients came straight from the very garden we had just contentedly strolled through made the estate's authentic farm-to-fork philosophy a truly special experience for us! While we adults delighted in browsing in the concept store, the highlight for our children was the encounters with animals: the gentle donkeys that loved being petted, the chickens, and those wonderful white ducks waddling mischievously everywhere. Babylonstoren felt wonderfully unhurried and deeply connected to nature for us all, especially during our boat trip at the dam, waters shimmering magically in the evening sun.

GROOTBOS

Wild and Vast

OCEAN SAFARIS TO THE "BIG FIVE" OF THE SEA, HORSEBACK RIDES THROUGH BLOOMING FYNBOS, DISCOVERY TOURS IN ONE OF THE MOST BIODIVERSE NATURAL PARADISES ON EARTH: THOSE IN SEARCH OF A SANCTUARY BETWEEN MOUNTAINS AND SEA WILL FIND IT AT GROOTBOS!

Opposite page: Wide sandy beaches framed by rugged rock formations characterize spectacular Walker Bay.

Above: The view from the Garden Lodge over the wooded mountain landscape and the bay is magnificent.

Right: Visiting the farm animals is always a highlight for children.

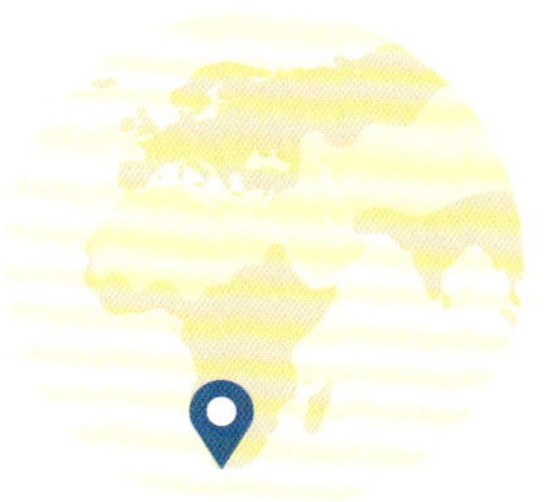

Where: Private nature reserve in southern South Africa, just under three hours southeast of Cape Town

What: 2 fynbos lodges with 27 suites
Vibe: Sustainable, welcoming, and in harmony with nature

The Garden Lodge's panorama deck is the perfect spot for evening drinks and sunset vibes.

Opposite page: Connect with nature on beach picnics and horseback rides through the fynbos.

Few places offer such a breathtaking variety of natural landscapes as Grootbos. This private nature reserve at the southern tip of South Africa is nestled in the country's colorful fynbos vegetation, which stretches from the mountain slopes down to the striking rock formations and sandy beaches of Walker Bay. Amid this untouched landscape, the elegant suites of the two lodges provide the utmost comfort along with incomparable ocean views from private decks.

At the Garden Lodge, everything is designed with families in mind: a large pool, diverse children's programs, and ample space to run and play while parents unwind in the spa. Guests can indulge in multi-course menus in the two lodge restaurants, or enjoy picnics on the beach or in the wilderness of the reserve.

Almost everything served at Grootbos is grown in the immediate surroundings—a double benefit, since it also helps train local residents in sustainable agriculture. A true highlight for the whole family is the bush dinner beneath a canopy of stars at the boma, the central open-air gathering place.

BETWEEN MOUNTAINS, FYNBOS, AND OCEAN

Young explorers love the abundance of wildlife at Grootbos, and beginners and advanced riders alike can explore the fynbos on horseback with experienced guides. The range of nature activities within this biodiverse reserve is impressive. On jeep tours or guided walks through the fynbos and ancient milkwood forests, visitors discover over 900 plant species, including South Africa's national flower, the protea. Pearly white beaches and mysterious caves beckon along the coast, and just offshore lies the chance to encounter the "Big Five" of the ocean: whales, sharks, dolphins, seals, and playful penguins. Spotting them up close by boat is an experience you will never forget!

HIGHLIGHTS FOR KIDS & TEENS:

- Beginner-friendly horseback rides through the fynbos
- Hands-on activities in the garden and with the smaller farm animals
- Picnic outings to the beach and exciting cave hikes
- Boat trips to see the "Big Five" of the ocean

ACTIVITIES OFFERED AT THE RESORT:

- Discover the fynbos on guided walks and botanical safaris
- Horseback rides with experienced guides
- Explore coastal caves and cliffs
- Learn about the Grootbos Foundation's local sustainability initiatives
- Relax with spa treatments
- Excellent restaurants with panoramic terraces

WHY WE LOVE IT—OUR FAMILY EXPERIENCE:

Grootbos felt like a home in the wilderness, nestled between ocean and mountains, surrounded by vast, tranquil openness. We were fortunate to celebrate New Year's Eve here, and we could not imagine a more beautiful place to welcome the year ahead. The excellent cuisine and warm, attentive service, with so many thoughtful details, allowed us adults to truly unwind, while our children delighted in discovering the animals, the vegetable garden, and the wonderful playground. The highlight was our marine safari, where we saw all of the "Big Five" of the ocean—whales, dolphins, seals, sharks, and penguins. Our horseback ride through the fynbos, a picnic on the beach framed by a spectacular coastline, a hike through mysterious caves, and that incredible view across Walker Bay that accompanied us everywhere: All of this made Grootbos one of the most special places we have ever been.

ZANNIER SONOP

The Great Wide Open

A DESERT ADVENTURE LIKE IN DAYS GONE BY: ZANNIER SONOP'S LUXURIOUS TENTED CAMP REVIVES BYGONE SPLENDOR WITH STYLE AND MODERN COMFORTS IN THE HEART OF ONE OF AFRICA'S MOST MAGNIFICENT NATURAL LANDSCAPES.

Where: On a wild rocky plateau in the far south of Namibia, in the Karas region

What: 10 luxurious tented suites for families with children 6 and up
Vibe: Adventurous with a historical touch, close to nature

Arriving at Zannier Sonop feels like stepping into a time machine that transports you straight into the adventure of a lifetime. This exclusive camp in southern Namibia sits sublimely atop a spectacular rocky plateau, commanding infinite views across the expanse, much like the opening scene of a classic blockbuster. Even the ten luxurious tent suites possess cinematic flair, with hand-knotted rugs, nostalgic steamer trunks, and telescopes from bygone eras making you feel as though you are following in the footsteps of an expedition, yet they are perfectly paired with contemporary amenities. It is an atmosphere suspended between reality and fiction, one that captivates travelers of all ages. Fitting this almost surreally composed setting, an infinity pool suddenly appears in the middle of it all, alongside spa and fitness facilities. Culinary traditions run deep at Zannier Sonop. Each evening brings an exquisite gala dinner celebrated with fine silverware, flickering candelabras, and refined butler service—transforming every meal into the day's crowning moment.

INFINITE SILENCE, STARRY SKIES

The desert adventure at Zannier Sonop unfolds in countless ways. Guided horseback rides delight the whole family, even those without riding experience. Those seeking action can explore by ebike or embark on a nature safari by jeep. Guided hikes train the eye to discover nature's small miracles at your feet. For moments of pure tranquility, the silence surrounding Zannier Sonop proves perfect: relaxing while gazing into the distance, drinks at sunset looking over the rocks, a walk bathed in magical early morning light that lends the colors of sand and stone an almost otherworldly enchantment. Zannier Sonop also lies within a dark sky zone, ideal for observing the star-studded night sky through a telescope or with the naked eye.

Previous pages: Beautiful, almost surreally so: Sonop's infinity pool with a magnificent view into the distance.

Opposite page: Nostalgic gala dinners bring back the splendor of days gone by.

Below left: Exploring the desert trails on an eFatBike.

Below right: Those who venture out on foot will discover with every step the small natural wonders hidden within the seemingly barren landscape.

HIGHLIGHTS FOR KIDS & TEENS:

- Horseback riding excursions through the desert landscape, beginners welcome
- Open-air movies under the stars
- The Southern Hemisphere's night sky: stargazing by telescope
- Exciting discovery tours by jeep

ACTIVITIES OFFERED AT THE RESORT:

- Guided tours on horseback or by ebike
- Stargazing through a telescope or with the naked eye
- Luxury picnics in the dunes and elegant afternoon tea
- Desert safaris by jeep and dinners in a vintage-style atmosphere
- Wellness treatments in the spa with seemingly endless views

WHY WE LOVE IT—OUR FAMILY EXPERIENCE:

Adventure and the glamour of bygone eras, a cinematic backdrop, this timeless atmosphere in the heart of the desert—Zannier Sonop completely swept us off our feet! We felt like we were part of a glamorous expedition from another era. Our luxurious tented suite served as a stylish base camp for unforgettable experiences: drinks at sundown amid dunes glowing red in the evening light, movie nights beneath the crystalline starry sky by the pool, eFatBike rides through the desert, elegant gala dinners with vintage charm—simply magical! Yet the true star at Zannier Sonop is the desert itself, surreal beauty composed of nothing but rock, light, and endless horizons that made us feel both humbly small and wonderfully alive!

ANDBEYOND SOSSUSVLEI DESERT LODGE

Under the Stars

ON THE EDGE OF THE NAMIB DESERT, THE FUTURISTIC SOSSUSVLEI DESERT LODGE OFFERS THE LUXURY OF EXPERIENCING NAMIBIA'S MOST SPECTACULAR DUNE LANDSCAPE IN COMPLETE PRIVACY: WITH A PRIVATE OBSERVATORY, ACTION-PACKED DESERT TOURS, AND SWEEPING PANORAMIC VISTAS OF THE INFINITE EXPANSE.

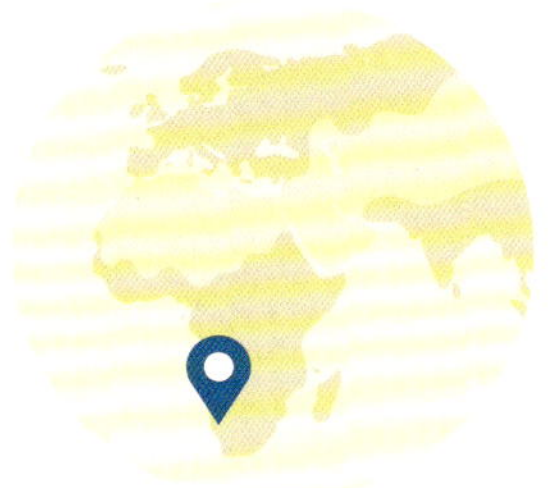

Where: In a private nature reserve in Namib-Naukluft National Park, a good hour's flight south of Windhoek

What: 12 panoramic suites with an abundance of privacy and comfort
Vibe: Stylish, extraordinary, full of experiences

The Namib is considered the oldest desert in the world, and the salt pans of Sossusvlei, surrounded by the highest dunes in Africa, are particularly impressive with their otherworldly beauty. At andBeyond Sossusvlei Desert Lodge, you are immersed in this surreal dream world of red sand. The extravagant suites, designed with steel, stone, and expansive glass, evoke the dune landscape while distinctively standing apart from it. In the almost 50-square-mile private reserve, you can enjoy luxury delivered sustainably. Solar panels produce energy for air conditioning and other comforts and power the lodge's water treatment and recycling systems. Every suite boasts spectacular desert landscape panoramas, and a skylight above the bed provides a literally heavenly view of the starry sky! The private pool on your very own terrace is perfect for cooling off after an active day.

THE NAMIB'S MOST BEAUTIFUL DUNES

The Desert Lodge offers its guests exclusive access to the spectacular natural wonders of the dune landscape, ensuring completely private desert adventures. Quiet moments alternate between solitary hikes or guided explorations with experienced geologists, and more active pursuits like ebike tours or thrilling quad bike excursions, where children who are old enough can even take the wheel themselves! Experience the sky over the Namib from every perspective: Soar above in a hot air balloon or helicopter for a breathtaking bird's-eye view of the landscape's unique beauty. Discover the clear night sky with our resident astronomer at the lodge's observatory—Sossusvlei Private Reserve is in one of the planet's best dark sky zones!

Previous page: Like stepping onto another planet—the lodge lies in the very heart of the desert (left). Here, luxury takes on a unique meaning: Slip into your private pool just outside the desert suite (right), or scale the highest dunes in solitude, feeling as though you have reached the edge of heaven (far right).

Below left and right: There are many ways to discover the desert in Sossusvlei—whether you are racing across the sands on a quad bike or soaring above the sweeping dune landscape in a helicopter.

HIGHLIGHTS FOR KIDS & TEENS:

- Quad bike adventures through the dunes for older children who meet the age requirements
- Stargazing through the telescope with the lodge's resident astronomer
- Creative learning: discovering the desert's fascinating wildlife and ecology
- Family picnic among the dunes

ACTIVITIES OFFERED AT THE RESORT:

- Quad biking, desert hikes, and helicopter tours over Sossusvlei
- The "Big Daddy" experience: climb the region's tallest dune
- Excursions to Deadvlei and Sesriem Canyon
- Sunset cocktails followed by a private dinner amid the dunes
- Spa treatments and yoga in the desert serenity

WHY WE LOVE IT—OUR FAMILY EXPERIENCE:

The architecture? Simply extraordinary! The dune landscape? Utterly spectacular! The atmosphere? Uniquely enchanting! The Sossusvlei Desert Lodge captivated us instantly, especially our accommodations. The Star Dune Suite was simply breathtaking—spacious, stylish, and with a seemingly endless view into the vastness beyond ... The activities offered the perfect variety for our entire family. We rode quad bikes through the dreamlike dune landscape, glowing golden in the evening sun, then sipped chilled cocktails at sunset amid the desert's timeless sand sculptures. While some of us conquered "Big Daddy," the Namib's tallest dune, others took to the skies in a helicopter, marveling at the landscape's magical beauty from above. Sossusvlei held the perfect moment for each of us, young and old alike—which is why we are sure to return to this fascinating place!

Above: The lodge's striking architecture features a futuristic aesthetic.

Right: The lodge's restaurant combines an elegant interior with sweeping views of the desert landscape.

WILDERNESS SERRA CAFEMA

Down by the River

HIDDEN ALONG THE KUNENE RIVER, IN THE HOMELAND OF THE HIMBA, LIES ONE OF NAMIBIA'S MOST REMOTE LODGES. SERRA CAFEMA IS A BEAUTIFUL WORLD OF CONTRASTS: TRANQUILITY AND ADVENTURE, DESERT AND WATER—AN EXCLUSIVE RETREAT, IDEAL FOR FAMILIES.

Where: In northwest Namibia, right on the Kunene River in the Kunene Region, bordering Angola

What: Chalets on platforms by the river, closely connected to nature
Vibe: cozy, sustainable, and relaxed

HIGHLIGHTS FOR KIDS & TEENS:

- Quad bike adventures through dunes and rocky desert terrain (age restrictions apply)
- Respectful and unforgettable cultural experiences with the Himba people
- Kunene River boat trips
- Exciting safaris through one of Africa's most dramatic landscapes

ACTIVITIES OFFERED AT THE CAMP:

- Guided quad bike tours through dunes, canyons, and dry riverbeds
- Boat trips along the Kunene with birdwatching
- Cultural encounters with the Himba community
- Hikes through the otherworldly, rocky Mars-like landscape
- Relaxing hours on your private deck overlooking the river valley

Opposite page: An exclusive green oasis by the river—Serra Cafema Lodge is comprised of just eight tented chalets.

Above left: The entire family zooms through the dunes on quad bikes.

Above right: Everyone pitches in when landing on the banks of the Kunene.

In Namibia's far northwest, the world grows hushed, and time itself seems to slow. Here, where barren desert meets the distinctive rock formations of the Angolan Rand Mountains, the Kunene River winds through a breathtaking landscape. Along this vital green lifeline lies a hidden oasis: Serra Cafema. Home to just eight tented chalets, this intimate camp provides genuine refuge, seamlessly merging modern luxury with the desert's minimalist beauty and traditional elements that pay homage to Himba culture. Perched on a riverside hill, the lodge's interconnected wooden decks and walkways offer sweeping views of the river valley from every vantage point.

ADVENTURE-PACKED BETWEEN RIVER AND DESERT

The camp's serene atmosphere belies the countless unique experiences that await. Glide past the lush Kunene riverbanks by boat or encounter oryx antelopes and desert chameleons on guided jeep excursions through the neighboring dunes, culminating in a leisurely picnic in the midst of this enchanting landscape. And when the whole family races across the dunes on quad bikes, excitement is guaranteed for all ages.

The Himba, a semi-nomadic people who see themselves as guardians of nature and wildlife, have lived in this region for centuries—and the camp considers itself a guest in their homeland. Just as the Himba generously share their culture and traditions with visitors, Serra Cafema supports the community with educational programs and medical care.

WHY WE LOVE IT—OUR FAMILY EXPERIENCE:

There are places that tell stories—and then there are places that write stories themselves. For us, Serra Cafema is one of Namibia's most fascinating lodges: secluded, authentic, and intense. Its spectacular location on the banks of the Kunene River offers stunning views into Angola. We traveled by boat to the border and crossed one of the country's pristine landscapes. During our visit to the Himba, we had the rare privilege of experiencing the culture and everyday life of this semi-nomadic people. Their openness made this respectful encounter deeply moving for all of us. We explored the rugged, otherworldly desert landscape, wild and infinitely vast, on a quad bike tour. Back at camp, comfort, coziness, and excellent cuisine awaited, along with a feeling of having arrived at the world's edge, in a truly special place.

Below: Serra Cafema offers a rare and respectful opportunity to personally engage with the culture and daily life of the semi-nomadic Himba people.

Above: The tented chalets are the perfect combination of traditional regional architecture and stylish, inviting interiors.

Left: The river landscape defines the essence of Serra Cafema.

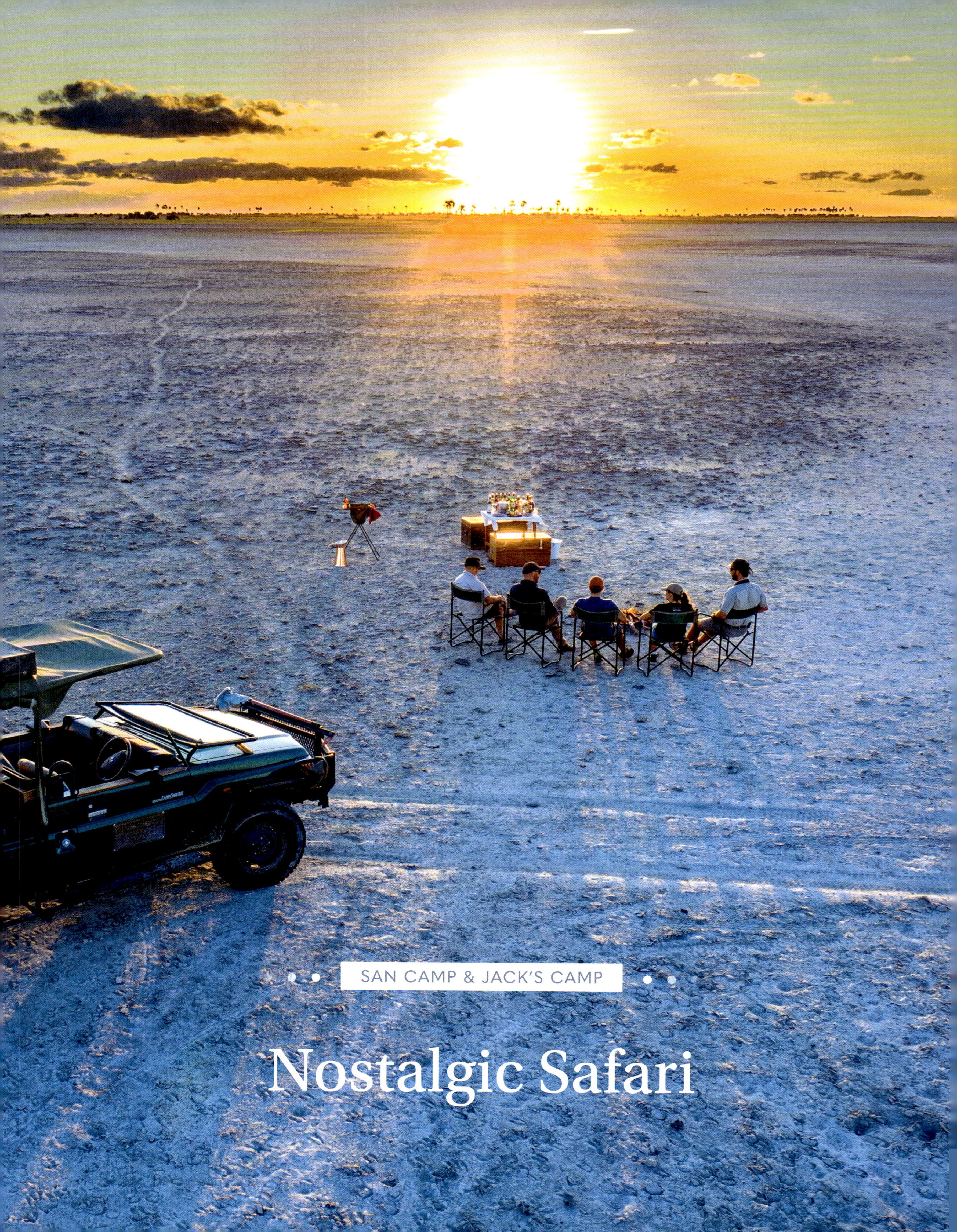

SAN CAMP & JACK'S CAMP

Nostalgic Safari

IN THE VASTNESS OF THE MAKGADIKGADI SALT PANS, SAN CAMP AND JACK'S CAMP WELCOME THEIR GUESTS WITH A BLEND OF MINIMALISM, NOSTALGIC GRANDEUR, AND A TOUCH OF ADVENTURE.

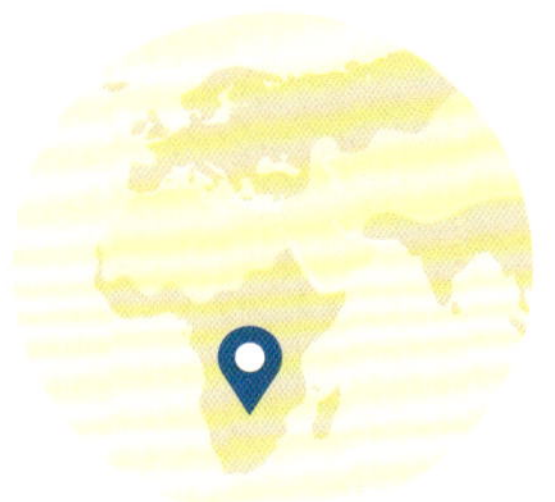

Where: At the Ntwetwe Pan in Makgadikgadi National Park, in Botswana's Central District

What: 2 stylish and exclusive tented camps
Vibe: Nostalgic, peaceful, and enchanting

Deep within the serene expanse of the Makgadikgadi salt pans, believed by paleontologists to be the cradle of humankind, extraordinary safari experiences await in two distinct forms. Though San Camp and Jack's Camp differ dramatically in style, both ignite the same passion for the magic of Botswana's endless horizons.

At Jack's Camp, modern luxury and a fascination for the bygone era go hand in hand. Enormous, lavishly furnished tents exude classic safari charm, immersing guests in the elegant world of 1940s exploration, complete with a pool under the tent roof. Every detail evokes the golden age of safari, while the fossil museum captivates visitors of all ages. San Camp, by contrast, is minimalist, bright, and almost ethereal. Romantic four-poster beds stand within open tent walls that sway gently with the breeze, offering uninterrupted views across the endless expanse of the Ntwetwe Pan.

OUT INTO THE SALT PANS

Both camps offer unique family experiences: whizzing across the vast Makgadikgadi salt pans on quad bikes, discovering the salt desert through the eyes of the local San on guided Bushman walks, and learning about local traditions such as fire-making and tracking. Encounters with the region's perhaps most endearing residents are unforgettable: The charming meerkats seem to befriend human visitors all on their own. When night falls, the desert magic continues with excursions into the salt pans, culminating in a night alone under the dazzling starry sky.

Previous page (left page): An evening cocktail in the salt desert rounds off the safari.

Previous page (right page): The open tents at San Camp convey a sense of freedom (right). The adorable bat-eared foxes, with their oversized ears, are perfectly adapted to the desert habitat (left).

Below left and right: Not only impressive for children—the Bushman walks with the Ju/'hoansi and the encounters with the friendly meerkats

ACTIVITIES OFFERED AT THE CAMP:

- Game drives with an impressive variety of animal sightings, such as lions, zebras, and wildebeest
- Bushman walks with the San
- Guided horseback rides
- Sleep beneath the stars in a comfortable bed under the open sky
- Seasonal highlights: zebra migration, elephant herds, and flamingo breeding colonies

HIGHLIGHTS FOR KIDS & TEENS:

- Encounter inquisitive meerkats remarkably close up
- Go on quad bike safaris across the salt pans
- Learn from the San: traditional fire-making and animal tracking
- Explore ancient fossils in the Jack's Camp museum

WHY WE LOVE IT—OUR FAMILY EXPERIENCE:

The white tents, the endless landscape, the golden light—the atmosphere of San Camp feels like a fairy tale! We experienced a world of contrasts by venturing far into the salt pan by quad bike, where, in the quiet magic of the desert, each of us was lost in quiet contemplation. The biggest surprise was our overnight expedition to the salt pan, where we slept warmly cocooned in camp beds directly beneath the starry heavens. Equally unforgettable was how the San welcomed us into their world, revealing the wonders of the Makgadikgadi through their eyes.

Above: Jack's Camp brings the glamorous safari era back to life.

Right: Opulence in the desert—the tea tent with Persian carpets at Jack's Camp.

An Oasis of Tranquility

AT THIS ICONIC CAMP, GUESTS EXPERIENCE THE OKAVANGO DELTA'S INCOMPARABLE BIODIVERSITY IN COMPLETE EXCLUSIVITY: VILLAS BENEATH A LUSH CANOPY, SWEEPING VIEWS ACROSS THE FLOODPLAINS—AND A FRIENDLY TEAM DELIVERING EXCEPTIONAL SAFARIS ON LAND AND WATER.

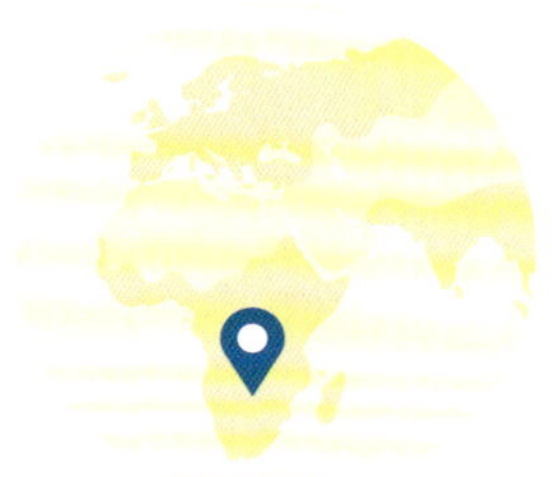

Where: In the Okavango Delta in Botswana's North-West District, 120 km (75 miles) as the crow flies from the district capital of Maun

What: 5 safari suites and 2 luxury villas for families
Vibe: Brilliantly designed and yet close to nature

The Okavango Delta stands as one of Africa's most captivating natural wonders. Each year, rainfall in Angola's highlands transforms northern Botswana's arid Kalahari basin into a thriving biodiversity paradise. Here, on a private island between the waterways within the exclusive Jao Reserve, lies a true oasis: Jao Camp. This architecturally stunning retreat is accessible only by light aircraft. Witnessing nature's metamorphosis as the silted delta becomes an intricate network of channels and lagoons after the rains is part of the special magic of Jao Camp. With just five suites and two villas, all elevated on stilts, the camp offers both privacy and an intimate connection with nature. The spacious accommodations with tented roofs and generous use of wood are ideal for families. Each boasts its own pool, lounge and dining area, plus plenty of space inside and on the decks, making them simultaneously airy and cozy. Artful design elements throughout the camp strike a perfect chord between rustic authenticity and refined elegance. The heart of the camp is its expansive lounge with sweeping views over the delta landscape. Alongside a spa that appears to float among the treetops and the elegant bar, it houses a small natural history museum, with a towering giraffe skeleton sure to catch your eye.

GO ON SAFARI WITH A PRIVATE CREW

Villa guests enjoy the exclusive services of a private butler, chef, and guide, with a dedicated vehicle for family game drives. Other highlights include guided bush walks and water-based explorations by boat. Alongside lion, leopard, elephant, and others, the delta's floodplains alone are home to some 930 bird species, and Jao Camp's private reserve is deeply committed to preserving this unique ecosystem.

HIGHLIGHTS FOR KIDS & TEENS:

- Guided nature experiences: tracking, bow and arrow carving, stargazing
- Glide through the channels in a mokoro dugout canoe, water levels permitting
- Wildlife viewing on water and land—seasonal highlights vary
- Ample space for children to play

ACTIVITIES OFFERED AT THE CAMP:

- Sleep beneath the stars on an elevated platform deep in the savanna
- Game drives, hikes, and birdwatching with expert guides
- Spa treatments and massages overlooking lush greenery
- Helicopter flights offering breathtaking aerial views of the delta

Left: Glide silently through the waterways by boat, surrounded by beautiful carpets of water lilies.

Above: Observe wildlife on foot with experienced guides.

Jao Camp excels at blending design and comfort.

Above: The villas are nestled in nature, where land and water converge.

Right: If you want to see a fascinating variety of wildlife, including leopards, the Okavango Delta is the place to be.

WHY WE LOVE IT—OUR FAMILY EXPERIENCE:

We experienced Jao Camp as a genuine oasis—so immersed in nature that the vitality of the Okavango Delta was palpable. Water levels rose daily, and we watched in wonder as the camp gradually became an island. This constant metamorphosis made every day feel utterly unique. Diverse wildlife gathered just beyond our veranda: elephants, lions, hippos, and an abundance of bird species you can only experience with such intensity here! Our mokoro excursions in traditional dugout canoes were an absolute highlight. We glided silently along narrow waterways through water lilies and papyrus. Our children still talk about learning the traditional art of fire-making from the locals. As for the camp itself? Its sophisticated, stylish elegance felt immediately welcoming—Jao struck the perfect balance between contemporary design and an authentic wilderness feeling.

Above: Surrounded by the leafy treetops, the lounge offers a vast view across the water.

Right: A room with a view—you can even watch the life on the water from the comfort of your bed.

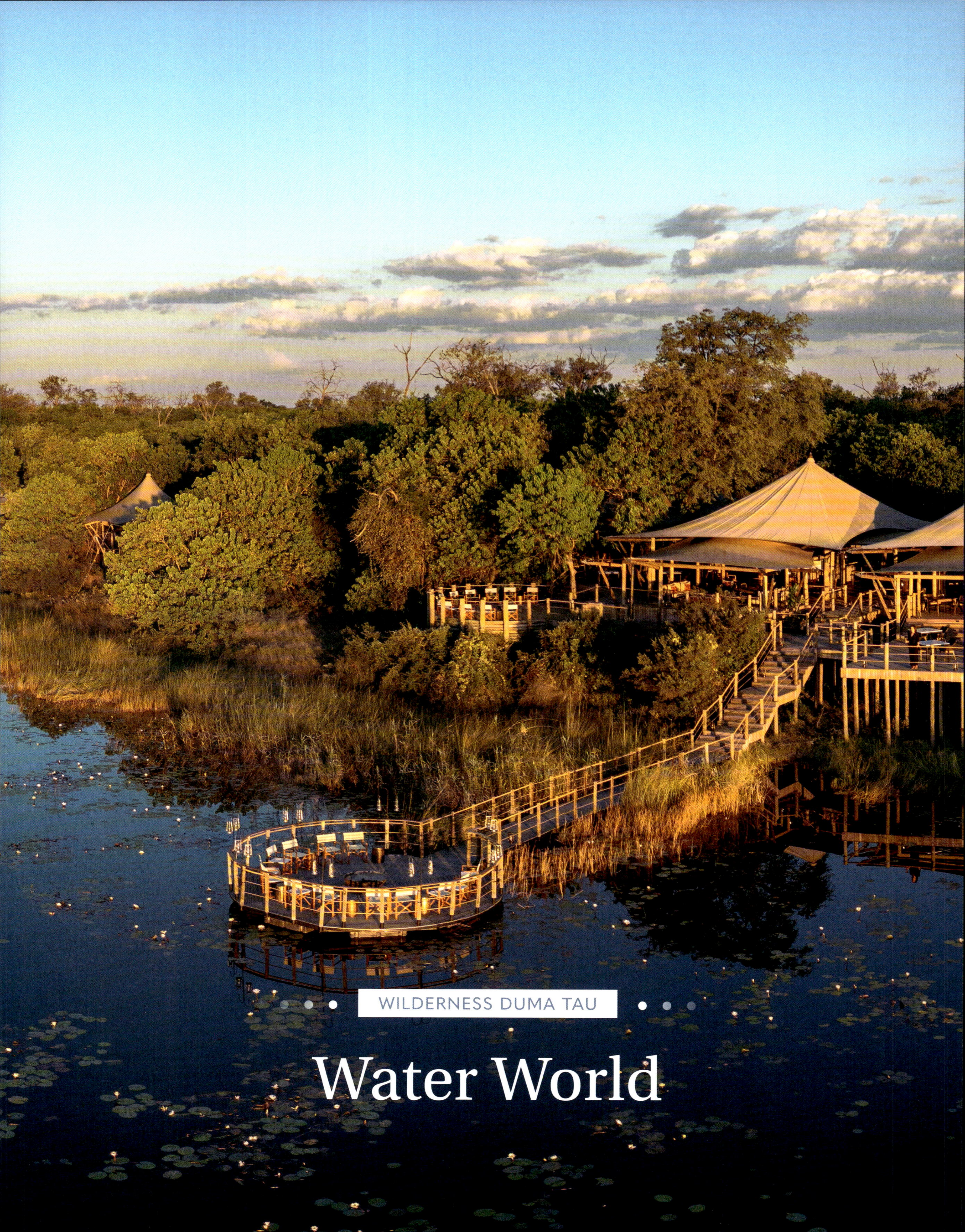

WILDERNESS DUMA TAU

Water World

IN THE ELEPHANT KINGDOM: THE EXCLUSIVE DUMA TAU TENTED CAMP OFFERS ENCOUNTERS WITH MIGHTY PACHYDERMS AT EVERY TURN, EVEN RIGHT OUTSIDE YOUR SUITE.

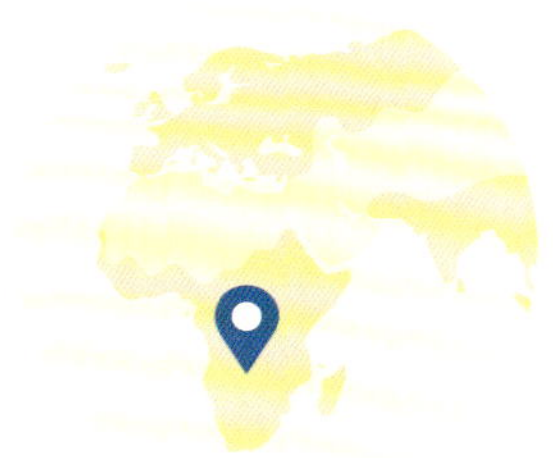

Where: On the Linyanti River in northern Botswana, on the border with Namibia

What: 8 spacious tented suites
Vibe: Right in nature, elegant, cozy

Duma Tau means "the roar of the lion" in Setswana—but although giraffes, wild dogs, and other animals roam this private Linyanti reserve alongside the king of the beasts, elephants are the true stars here. The camp lies nestled between heavily frequented migratory corridors of two of Africa's largest elephant populations, whose protection is at the heart of this sustainably managed reserve. You don't even have to step outside your suite at Duma Tau to experience these majestic giants up close. From the decks of the luxurious tent suites, guests enjoy sweeping views across the Osprey Lagoon, a favorite watering spot of the herds.

LODGE WITH LAGOON VIEWS

Perched on raised wooden platforms, the carefully chosen accommodations combine wood, canvas, light, and spaciousness to create an elegant atmosphere of well-being. The large family suite is an ideal retreat for guests with children, complete with a private pool on the wooden deck, perfect for cooling off while soaking in the beauty of the surroundings. A larger swimming pool, gym, and spa add to the comforts, while the restaurant on a viewing platform above the water impresses with both its location and its superior cuisine. Young nature explorers become little trackers, learning from the guides about animal behavior and the secrets of the wild. On safaris in open jeeps or by boat, families experience a rich variety of wildlife and waterbirds from new perspectives.

Giraffes also use the lagoon right next to the camp as a watering hole.

Previous pages: Dinner at sunset—the lodge restaurant's jetty extends out into the lagoon.

Below left: Nowhere else will you see elephants as close as at Duma Tau.

Below right: Splashing in the expansive main pool—the perfect refreshment after an action-packed safari day.

ACTIVITIES OFFERED AT THE CAMP:

- Game drives in open safari vehicles
- Birdwatching, especially during migration season
- Nature walks with experienced guides
- Boat trips with picnics and drinks at sunset
- Relaxation in the pool or spa overlooking the lagoon

HIGHLIGHTS FOR KIDS & TEENS:

- Elephant watching right from your own deck
- Boat tours on the Linyanti River
- Learning with guides: tracking and discovering the secrets of the bush
- Family-friendly suites with pools, plenty of space, and privacy

WHY WE LOVE IT—OUR FAMILY EXPERIENCE:

Elephants everywhere, and so close: At Duma Tau, we found one of the best places in Africa to experience these magnificent animals in all their glory, from many different perspectives. Not only from the safari jeep but also right from our villa: We watched entire herds crossing the river—calm, majestic, and just a few feet away! Then, on our boat trip, we encountered lone bull elephants bathing and drinking in the water—powerful, peaceful, and silent. It was a sight we will never forget.

In the Realm of "the Smoke that Thunders"

TWO WORLDS, EQUALLY SPECTACULAR: THE LODGE ON THE ZAMBEZI'S SOUTH BANK OFFERS PRISTINE WILDLIFE ENCOUNTERS, WHILE THE MIGHTY VICTORIA FALLS THUNDERS CLOSE BY.

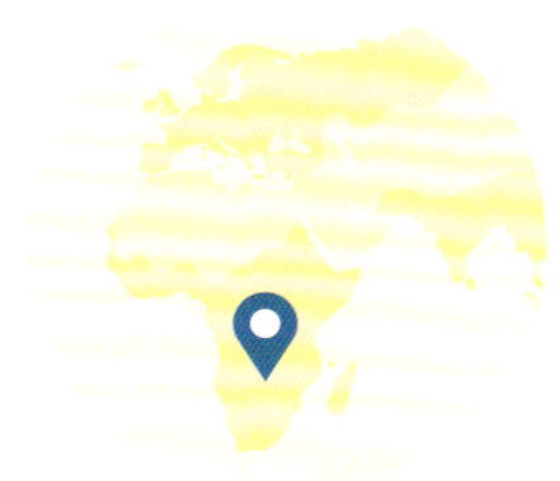

Where: On the banks of the Zambezi in northern Zimbabwe, on the border with Zambia

What: 18 suites directly on the river
Vibe: Designed with Zimbabwean inspiration, very family-friendly

Left: Dinner out in the bush under the trees, with the lanterns and a fire bowl creating an enchanting atmosphere.

Opposite page, top: The patios of the private villas overlooking the Zambezi are perfect for relaxing.

Opposite page, bottom: The stylish suites all have their own outdoor spaces and private pools.

HIGHLIGHTS FOR KIDS & TEENS:

- Visit Victoria Falls on foot and by helicopter
- Safari with experienced guides in our own reserve
- For daring teenagers: gorge swinging, bungee jumping, and the flying fox
- Whitewater rafting and swimming in the Devil's Pool right on the edge of the waterfalls

ACTIVITIES OFFERED AT THE RESORT:

- Private game drives in an open vehicle day and night
- Boat safaris and sunset cruises on the Zambezi
- Helicopter flights over Victoria Falls
- Visits to local markets and discovery of local craftsmanship
- Exquisite gourmet dinners by Zimbabwe's most renowned chefs

Above: The helicopter flight to the waterfalls is an unforgettable adventure that children will treasure for a long time to come.

Go on safari to see four of the Big Five and the largest waterfalls in the world on a single trip. It is this spectacular combination that makes a stay at Matetsi Victoria Falls truly extraordinary. The lodge maintains a 135,000-acre game reserve, safeguarding not only the wildlife of the savanna but also the ecosystems along its private nine-mile stretch of the Zambezi. The 18 suites, including two designed especially for families, combine contemporary design with a Zimbabwean touch while remaining deeply connected to their impressive natural surroundings. Each has a private patio and pool with views of the river that never get boring. Family suites give children their own space yet keep them close to their parents, and the spa offers treatments that feel in tune with nature itself. Evenings are unforgettable at the open-air boma, where lanterns and fire bowls set the stage for exquisite gourmet dinners beneath the stars.

BUFFALO HERDS, ELEPHANTS, LIONS, AND THE WORLD'S LARGEST WATERFALLS

There are several ways to experience the biodiversity and secrets of the bush in the company of experienced guides: bush walks, game drives in an open jeep, or by boat on the river. Vast herds of buffalo and elephants are breathtaking to observe, cheeky warthogs often wander through camp, and large prides of lions may even be spotted along the banks of the Zambezi. The highlight, of course, is the proximity to the Victoria Falls, just 30 miles away. A scenic helicopter flight over the thundering cascade of water is an adventure children will never forget. On foot, a personal guide can lead you close to the very edge of the falls, where, standing in the mist of the roaring spray, you understand why the locals call this natural wonder Mosi-oa-Tunya, meaning "the smoke that thunders."

Above: The wild river landscape of the Zambezi boasts incredible biodiversity.

Right and far right: Guests at Matetsi Victoria Falls can also experience the spectacular sight of Victoria Falls on foot.

WHY WE LOVE IT—OUR FAMILY EXPERIENCE:

Matetsi Victoria Falls is wild and relaxed, elegant and full of possibilities. For us, the combination of an exclusive wildlife reserve with direct access to Victoria Falls was absolutely unique. The helicopter flight over the churning masses of water was a spectacular experience for all our children, and the excitement continued on the ground right by the waterfalls. Our brave teenagers ventured into the gorge on a kind of bungee jump—an experience they will remember for a long time to come! By contrast, our sunset cruise on the Zambezi was very serene and relaxed. As we glided through the golden light of late afternoon, gin and tonics in hand, we watched as hippos gathered for their own evening rendezvous very close by. Throughout our stay, we were pampered with culinary delights. The cuisine was inventive, fresh, and world-class. Above all, the professional team at Matetsi Victoria Falls took excellent care of us.

TIME & TIDE CHONGWE

Where the Rivers Meet

TWO MIGHTY RIVERS, SELECT TENTED SUITES AND A FASCINATING ABUNDANCE OF WILDLIFE—TIME & TIDE CHONGWE CAMP IS ALWAYS READY TO DELIVER SAFARI ADVENTURES THAT UNFOLD ANEW EACH DAY.

Where: In southern Zambia on the border with Zimbabwe, where the smaller Chongwe River flows into the mighty Zambezi

What: 4 rooms and 8 luxury tents overlooking the river panorama
Vibe: Stylish design and relaxed comfort, very private

At the confluence of the Chongwe and Zambezi rivers on the outskirts of Zambia's Lower Zambezi National Park sits the picturesque Time & Tide Chongwe Camp, directly on the water's edge. This pristine reserve offers a magnificent panorama and extraordinary wildlife diversity—everything you could wish for in an African wilderness camp. Whether you choose the exclusive Chongwe River House, a private four-bedroom family villa, or one of eight tented suites, the stylish accommodations radiate authentic African character with every modern comfort. The view of the river and across to the mountains of Zimbabwe on the other side never ceases to amaze. At the main lodge along with its bar and restaurant, a large pool beckons—a favorite retreat for both children and adults at the end of adventure-filled days. Occasionally, elephants wander into camp while guests are enjoying a drink at sunset on the terrace.

FLEXIBLE EXPERIENCES ON YOUR OWN SCHEDULE

Chongwe Camp offers round-the-clock wildlife encounters. Early morning or evening game drives reveal the savanna's nocturnal creatures, while guided canoe excursions explore the river's tranquil waterways. Boat safaris along the Zambezi rank among Chongwe's highlights, with regular sightings of elephants, hippos, crocodiles, and countless bird species. Bush walks with expert guides provide particularly intimate experiences. On foot, you will discover the national park's smaller, often-overlooked natural wonders. For children, tracking becomes an engaging adventure that teaches the vital importance of nature and wildlife conservation through hands-on experience. Ideal for families with younger children: Chongwe's safari activities adapt flexibly to individual needs and schedules.

Previous page: Unexpected visitors—elephants sometimes stop for a drink at Chongwe House's inviting pool.

Opposite page: Bathed in light and stylishly appointed, the tented suites at Chongwe Lodge sit directly on the riverbank.

Below left: Our first fishing adventure on the Zambezi.

Below right: Exploring the river by canoe with experienced guides offers a whole new perspective on nature and wildlife.

ACTIVITIES OFFERED AT THE CAMP:

- Game drives timed perfectly for day and night wildlife viewing
- New safari perspectives by boat on the Zambezi
- Canoe tours on the Chongwe River
- Bird watching and safari walks with experienced nature guides

HIGHLIGHTS FOR KIDS & TEENS:

- Canoe trips accompanied by expert guides
- First-time fishing experiences during river excursions
- Walking safaris and game drives in search of elephants, leopards, and African wild dogs
- Wildlife spotting directly from camp

WHY WE LOVE IT—OUR FAMILY EXPERIENCE:

Chongwe captivated us with its diversity—and its unbeatable location at the confluence of the Chongwe and Zambezi rivers. Each day brought mesmerizing wildlife theater visible right from our tented suite: buffalo herds moving along the far shore, elephants crossing the river, and so many grunting hippos emerging from the depths! Chongwe's variety was astounding: gliding silently through waterways by canoe in the morning, fishing on the river at midday, then tracking lions, leopards, and African wild dogs on evening game drives. No two days were the same, and that is what makes this place so vibrant and fascinating!

True Wilderness on the Luangwa

AT THIS EASTERN ZAMBIAN RESORT, ELEGANT DESIGN MEETS UNTAMED WILDERNESS. SPACIOUS TENTED SUITES OFFER FAMILIES FRONT-ROW ACCESS TO SOUTH LUANGWA NATIONAL PARK'S REMARKABLE WILDLIFE.

Where: In South Luangwa National Park, on the west bank of the eponymous river in eastern Zambia

What: 6 spacious, comfortable tented suites with their own decks and pools
Vibe: Utterly relaxed, the ideal combination of pure nature and refined comfort

Few places in Africa boast wildlife populations as dense as South Luangwa National Park—making Time & Tide Chinzombo the perfect base for encountering wild cats, giraffes, lions, elephants, buffalo, and hippos.

The lodge features just six riverside tented villas, including one exclusive family residence, ensuring complete privacy. Its philosophy blends pure wilderness with exceptional comfort and elegant design—from freestanding luxury bathtubs to chandeliers suspended in the tented suites. Living spaces flow seamlessly onto verandas with private plunge pools; from your terrace, you can watch elephants and hippos grazing along the banks. For the ultimate experience, swap your villa for a night beneath the stars: enjoy sunset cocktails by the campfire, then drift off under the starry sky until dawn's gentle light awakens a new day—simply magical!

SAFARIS ON LAND AND ON WATER

South Luangwa is also known as the "Valley of the Leopard," and from Chinzombo you can follow these wild cats through their habitat at their natural pace. The lodge offers both day and night game drives with expert guides who orchestrate unforgettable wildlife encounters. Walking safaris reveal another dimension entirely—children and adults alike are excited to learn traditional tracking techniques and animal behavior insights. While the dry season provides optimal wildlife viewing between river and savanna, the green season offers its own magic. When the Luangwa swells with rain, sunset boat trips combined with exquisite drinks become an extraordinary experience. Over 450 bird species are native to this wilderness of almost 3,560 square miles, protected and maintained by the Time & Tide Foundation.

HIGHLIGHTS FOR KIDS & TEENS:

- Watch hippos, elephants, and more directly from your tented suite
- Thrilling game drives with expert guides
- Learn with rangers: animal tracking, bird calls, and wildlife behavior
- Daily river crossings add adventure to every day
- Boat safaris on the Luangwa (seasonal)
- Private pool overlooking the river

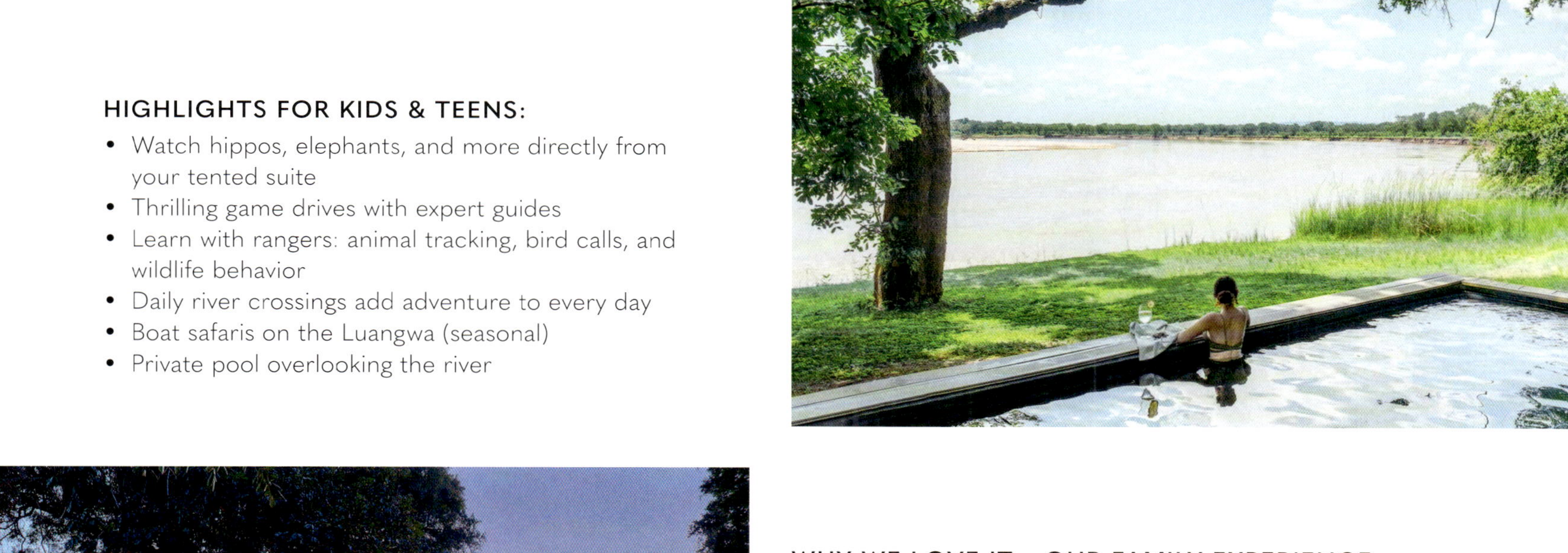

WHY WE LOVE IT – OUR FAMILY EXPERIENCE:

In the vast plains of South Luangwa, between lush river landscapes and gnarled ebony trees, we felt as though we were traveling deep into an untouched, almost mythical Africa. Time & Tide Chinzombo combines an ambiance of elegant design with intense nature experiences in its opulent tented suites. We will never forget relaxedly waking up to the sounds of the wild in our luxurious tent—and then, just moments later, catching sight of hippos grazing contentedly right by our veranda!

Left, top to bottom: The elegant, spacious family suites deliver every comfort imaginable. The stylish heart of camp—featuring lounge, library, and lush green views—provides the perfect sanctuary after open-vehicle safaris.

Right, top to bottom: Enjoy the panoramic view of the Luangwa from the pool at your family suite. The abundance of animals in this private nature reserve is truly impressive—even rare Crawshay's zebras roam these grounds.

Preserving Africa's Essence

PROTECTING NATURE AND BIODIVERSITY WHILE EMBRACING ECONOMIC RESPONSIBILITY: AT SEGERA, JOCHEN ZEITZ PROVES HOW TRAVEL CAN DRIVE SUSTAINABILITY.

Once the youngest CEO in Germany's sporting goods industry, Jochen Zeitz made a name for himself in the business world and later successfully guided the legendary motorcycle brand Harley-Davidson through its crisis. Yet his true life's work began with his first journey into the vast wilderness of Kenya. "I immediately caught the Africa virus. I have traveled to every continent, but it was Kenya that stole my heart." And that had its consequences. Zeitz didn't want to experience Kenya as a visitor, he wanted to live there, to immerse himself fully in its natural and cultural richness. In 2005 he impulsively decided to purchase a neglected cattle farm. Today, Segera is not only an exclusive retreat but also a 20,000-hectare (almost 50,000-acre) private nature reserve devoted to protecting the critically endangered black rhino. Working with the Zeitz Foundation and local communities, he launched an ambitious project to restore the degraded land around Segera. So far, 1.3 million native trees have been planted. The foundation trains female rangers to combat poaching and, in 2025, successfully reintroduced a founder population of black rhinos to the reserve—an important milestone for African conservation. "When you protect the rhino, you protect the entire ecosystem," says Zeitz.

CONSERVATION, COMMUNITY, CULTURE, COMMERCE

The philosophy of the "4 Cs"—conservation, community, culture, and commerce—is the foundation of Zeitz's comprehensive approach. He sees these as the cornerstones of all sustainable initiatives, designed to benefit both people and nature, because "only ecological business practices are profitable in the long term." The seasoned CEO understands the crucial interaction between ecological and economic transformation, insistent that business must be part of the equation. "Sustainability is no longer about doing less

Hands-on ranch life: Jochen Zeitz's children are also allowed to pitch in at Segera Farm.

harm, but about doing more good," he explains. "Charity is, of course, important. But since business accounts for more than 70 percent of environmental impact, it's up to business to find the solutions." At Segera, the heart of his vision, Zeitz brings all these threads together: nature conservation, social and cultural commitment, and economic responsibility. Along with his home in Santa Fe, the lodge is his and his family's second home. His children are growing up amid the wilderness of Kenya, experiencing the warmth of the local community and the beauty of Africa's nature. For Zeitz, it is the great joy of late fatherhood that enables him to be deeply present in their lives here. His daughter and son experience Segera's sustainability projects firsthand and naturally absorb respect for nature and the local people and culture. "Segera is a platform where I can make my experiences of Africa accessible to others," says Zeitz. At the same time, he emphasizes that the resort and the reserve must work hand in hand: "You cannot maintain such a place sustainably without the financial means to do so." For him, the resort is an important employer that enables the local community to live more sustainably.

A PLATFORM FOR AFRICAN ART

Thanks to Zeitz, African art also has a home on his reserve. The green gardens and open spaces around the lodge host an extensive collection of contemporary African installations and sculptures. He aims to make Segera a showcase for African art, strengthening its recognition in the international art world. With the founding of Zeitz MOCAA, Cape Town's Museum of Contemporary Art Africa, he offers artists across the continent a platform for visibility. He believes it is fundamentally wrong that outsiders have continued to define the view of Africa so far. "Here, Africa's artists can present themselves and tell their own stories."

Kenya's Sustainable Oasis of Art

SEGERA BRINGS AN EXTRAORDINARY VISION TO LIFE IN THE HEART OF THE SAVANNA: FAMILY-FRIENDLY SAFARI EXPERIENCES AND INDIVIDUAL LUXURY GO HAND IN HAND WITH NATURE AND WILDLIFE CONSERVATION, SOCIAL INITIATIVES, AND A UNIQUE CULTURAL EXPERIENCE.

Where: Private nature reserve on Kenya's Laikipia Plateau, around 155 miles north of the capital Nairobi

What: Houses and garden villas with a view of Mount Kenya
Vibe: In the heart of nature, dedicated, individual, and tailor-made

In the middle of the steppe-like wilds of Laikipia Plateau lies a lush, green oasis. Segera Retreat is the heart of a 20,000-hectare (almost 50,000-acre) private reserve dedicated to protecting nature and wildlife—above all, the endangered black rhino. Dense, flowering cacti form a typical *boma*, a kind of natural enclosure that creates a private sanctuary for families. Only a handful of luxurious villas, some raised on stilts with sweeping views, are scattered amid luxuriant gardens and a dreamlike pool area, serving as the exclusive base for exciting safaris. On private game drives with knowledgeable guides, guests encounter lions, elephants, leopards, cheetahs, and even the rare Grevy's zebra. With no set schedule, activities unfold at each family's own rhythm, making it ideal for those with young children. And sometimes there is no need to get into a vehicle at all: Watching a family of giraffes pass by the lodge on their way to the waterhole is part of everyday life at Segera. As the sun sets, the distant roar of lions echoes across Laikipia Plateau.

LUXURY MEETS RESPONSIBILITY

Segera considers itself more than just a socially responsible nature reserve, it is also a platform to showcase works by African artists. Before being exhibited at the MOCAA in Cape Town, inspiring paintings and sculptures can be admired throughout the gardens and lodge—up close and without museum barriers. Guests are invited to experience all aspects of the retreat's ecological and socially responsible philosophy: pioneering wildlife conservation, sustainable operations powered by solar energy and water recycling, and community projects that empower local people.

HIGHLIGHTS FOR KIDS & TEENS:

- Warm, caring hospitality that makes anything possible for children
- Creative workshops between game drives
- Sustainability programs explained in a child-friendly way
- Ranger tours: tracking animal footprints and birdwatching

ACTIVITIES OFFERED AT THE RESORT:

- Game drives through the wildlife-rich Laikipia region, horseback rides, and guided bush walks
- Discover contemporary African art in the extensive on-site gallery
- Learn about local community programs and foundation projects
- Wellness and yoga surrounded by nature
- Helicopter excursions and stargazing

Left: The Nay Palad Bird Nest is the perfect place for daydreams or a night under the open sky.

Top right: The spacious pool oasis offers a refreshing escape from the heat.

Above: Heartfelt exchanges with members of the local community.

Above: Segera emerged as a lush garden oasis in the heart of the savanna.

Opposite page, top: Works by African artists are exhibited here first before being shown at MOCAA in Cape Town.

Opposite page, bottom left: Segera specifically trains women in wildlife conservation and anti-poaching efforts.

Opposite page, bottom right: The pool villas offer families a private sanctuary with views of the wild.

WHY WE LOVE IT—OUR FAMILY EXPERIENCE:

What impressed us most about Segera was the remarkable sense of generosity and heartfelt warmth. On our son's birthday, we were treated to a celebration beyond anything we could have imagined—the enthusiasm of the entire staff was simply infectious. The children were attentively cared for at all times, making traditional beaded jewelry, splashing about in the pool oasis, and learning about sustainability projects through play. Alongside the powerful art experience at Segera Retreat, another highlight for us was visiting the local community. The Zeitz Foundation, which brings together education, entrepreneurship, and sustainability, empowers women to support their families and communities by producing handmade crafts or by training as rangers. Every meal was a highlight in itself: freshly prepared exactly as we desired and always served in new and memorable settings—as a picnic in the wild, in the former stables turned art gallery, or on a spectacular viewing platform overlooking the landscape.

Breakfast with Giraffes

THE NAME SAYS IT ALL. AT WHAT IS LIKELY KENYA'S OLDEST BOUTIQUE HOTEL, GIRAFFES ARE THE STARS. THE CHARMING SETTING IS PICTURE-PERFECT—CROWNED BY UNFORGETTABLE WILDLIFE ENCOUNTERS AT THE BREAKFAST TABLE!

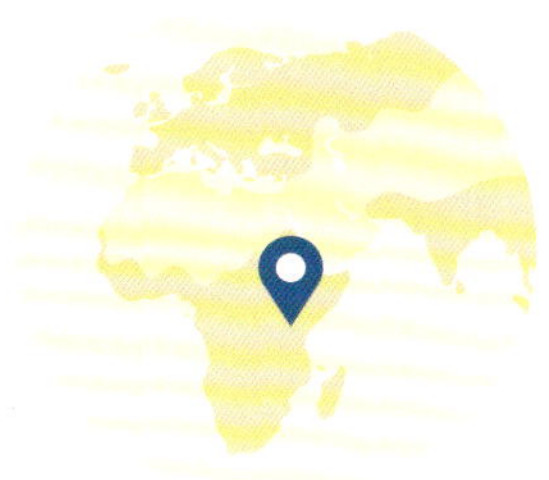

Where: Just outside Kenya's capital Nairobi, in the leafy suburb of Langata

What: 12 stylishly appointed rooms on a historic estate
Vibe: Unconventional, warm, and family-friendly

A hotel where giraffes stop by the breakfast table? It sounds bizarre, yet at Giraffe Manor on the outskirts of Nairobi, it is just everyday life. Built in 1932, the estate feels transported from another century—part Scottish hunting lodge, part *Out of Africa* setting. The original Manor House and the more modern Garden Manor each have six elegant rooms, blending modern luxury with African character and historical charm. Whether you are beginning a safari adventure from Nairobi or seeking a grand finale to your East African journey, this exceptional property deserves a place on your itinerary.

VISITING BABY ELEPHANTS

Giraffes appear everywhere here, as artistic motifs throughout the interiors and, more thrillingly, as living residents in the gardens. The estate's park-like nature reserve is home to a herd of endangered Nubian giraffes, who regularly visit the houses, particularly at breakfast time when they delicately extend their heads through open windows, seeking grass pellets. The sensation of their gentle lips taking food from your palm is deeply moving. The herd also likes to frequent afternoon tea on the terrace—feeding these trusting creatures from the garden's grand swing ranks among the highlights!

In addition to Nairobi's museums and conservation projects, the nearby elephant orphanage run by the Sheldrick Wildlife Trust also warrants a visit. Here, rescued baby elephants are lovingly nurtured, and visitors watch them have their milk feed and play in the mud—a wonderful experience!

Stylish and romantic, dinner by moonlight on the Manor House terrace.

Previous pages: Giraffes up close? Just outside Nairobi, this dream becomes reality.

Below left: Diving into the resort's pool offers the perfect refreshment after a trip into the hustle and bustle of Nairobi.

Below right: Feeding free-roaming giraffes by hand is an incredible experience!

HIGHLIGHTS FOR KIDS & TEENS:

- Feed giraffes directly through the window or in the gardens
- Visit rescued elephants at the elephant orphanage
- Explore the estate's gardens under child-friendly supervision while observing wildlife
- Excursion to a safari park, animal and nature conservation projects

ACTIVITIES OFFERED AT THE MANOR:

- Discover Nairobi National Park and its conservation initiatives
- For *Out of Africa* enthusiasts: the Karen Blixen Museum
- Unwind in the gardens or enjoy afternoon tea alongside the resident animals
- Explore Nairobi: small boutiques, local arts and crafts, markets and museums

WHY WE LOVE IT—OUR FAMILY EXPERIENCE:

Giraffe Manor was a fascinating experience for all of us. It is hard to imagine how much fun our youngest had feeding the giraffes—and when they suddenly poked their heads through the windows at breakfast looking for little tidbits, the amazement was complete! The animals are treated with respect and affection, and families immediately feel embraced by the warm hospitality. Nairobi itself surprised us too, especially the elephant orphanage visit, where we witnessed baby elephant care firsthand—an educational, emotional, and beautiful encounter!

A Rhino Paradise at Mount Kenya

SOLIO LODGE IS A TRANQUIL HIDEAWAY IN THE HEART OF A PRIVATE RHINO SANCTUARY, OFFERING EXCEPTIONAL WILDLIFE, WARM HOSPITALITY, AND MESMERIZING VIEWS OF MOUNT KENYA.

Where: In the private Solio Game Reserve between Mount Kenya and the Aberdare Mountains, 125 miles north of Nairobi

What: 5 luxurious cottages with open fireplaces
Vibe: Exclusive and stylish, with plenty of privacy and friendly hospitality

Nestled between the forested Aberdare slopes and the panorama of snow-capped Mount Kenya, Solio Lodge is the heart of the vast game reserve that bears the same name, and also the sole accommodation there. With just six cottages, complete privacy is assured. Their bright, uncluttered architecture combines traditional elements like thatched roofs with contemporary design. Expansive panoramic windows maintain your connection to nature while you enjoy the warmth of an open fireplace and a luxurious bathroom with freestanding tub.

A SAFE PLACE FOR ENDANGERED RHINOS

The 45,000-acre wildlife reserve is one of the most successful rhino conservation projects. Over 200 black and white rhinos now thrive here in the reserve, safe from poachers, and visitors can often see a herd of up to 40 animals together, a breathtaking experience unlikely to be found anywhere else. Guest contributions directly support Solio's conservation and breeding programs and fund community initiatives. A visit to a local school provides an opportunity for younger guests to connect. There is so much to see and do around Solio. On safari, you can discover the abundance of wildlife, from lions, leopards, zebras, and giraffes to a variety of antelope species. Depending on the time of day, breakfast or cocktails at sunset in the bush rounds off this wonderful experience. The surrounding landscape invites exploration on foot, by mountain bike, or on horseback, and a visit to a coffee farm offers fascinating insights. Mount Kenya's impressive silhouette can be seen for miles across the valley. For a change in perspective, you won't want to miss the opportunity to take a helicopter flight and experience the landscape from above.

HIGHLIGHTS FOR KIDS & TEENS:

- Exciting game drives with guaranteed rhino sightings, entirely on your own schedule
- Close encounters with a diversity of species guided by knowledgeable trackers
- Enthusiastic staff who inspire children's love of nature and the bush
- Picnics, horseback riding, flashlight hikes, and plenty of space to burn off energy

ACTIVITIES OFFERED AT THE RESORT:

- Explore the bush on horseback, on foot, or by mountain bike
- Helicopter flights to Mount Kenya or the Aberdare Mountains
- Get to know the country and its people by visiting local schools and markets
- Mobile safari bar for sunset drinks in the wild
- Fireside spa treatments

Above left: Rooftop seats on 4x4 vehicles offer the best view on game drives.

Left: Fresh produce is harvested from the organic garden and served in the restaurant.

Above: Friendly staff and a visit to the horses— young guests are warmly welcomed everywhere!

Thanks to the conservation program, over 200 black and white rhinos now live on Solio Game Reserve.

WHY WE LOVE IT—OUR FAMILY EXPERIENCE:

We were deeply moved by the warmth of the Solio Lodge team—especially our Maasai guide, who was affectionately dubbed "friend man" by our young son. His humorous nature immediately captured the hearts of our boys, making him a treasured companion throughout our stay. The rhino encounters in Solio are unique the world over. We had the opportunity to observe both white and black rhinos at close range—often in amazingly large groups, in the golden light of the savanna. That magical moment on the plateau when zebras, antelopes, and rhinos grazed peacefully side by side remains vivid in our memories. And then the breathtaking view of Mount Kenya, changing color with the time of day, powerful, sublime, majestic. In the stylish, welcoming ambiance of our spacious family suite with crackling fireplace and sweeping windows, we felt instantly at home.

Above: The architecture successfully blends traditional design and modern elements like the dramatic glass façade.

Right: Luxuriously appointed bathrooms invite complete relaxation.

Between the Serengeti and Ngorongoro

ANIMAL ENCOUNTERS AT SUNRISE, DINNERS IN THE BUSH, AND HELICOPTER FLIGHTS OVER THE SAVANNA: THE ELEGANT LEGENDARY EXPEDITIONS – MWIBA LODGE IN TANZANIA OFFERS BESPOKE SAFARIS THAT COMBINE MOMENTS OF TRANQUILITY WITH EXTRAORDINARY EXPERIENCES.

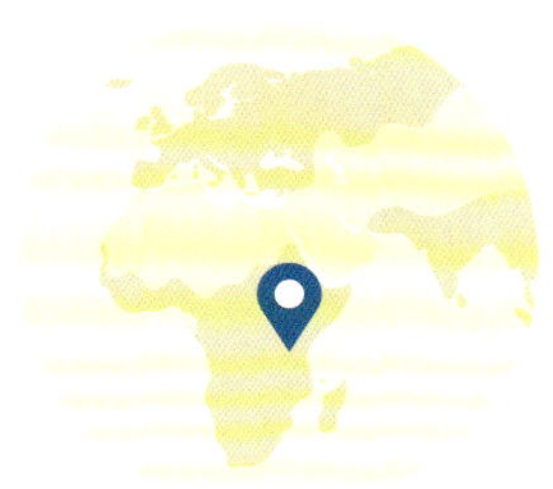

Where: Exclusive location in the private Mwiba Game Reserve in Tanzania, just south of the Serengeti

What: 10 spacious suites with a deck built on the rocks
Vibe: Close to nature with an adventurous touch

Left: During game drives, hippos can be seen taking a cooling dip at the waterholes.

Opposite page, top left and right: The jacuzzi in the rocks and the lodge's deck offer spectacular views.

Opposite page, bottom: The wooden pool deck provides the perfect spot to view the sunset.

HIGHLIGHTS FOR KIDS & TEENS:

- Lovingly guided bush walks with tracking and nature education
- Swimming in the rock pool with a sweeping view
- Adventure picnics in a wilderness setting
- Carving workshops with local guides

ACTIVITIES OFFERED AT THE RESORT:

- Day and night game drives and guided walking safaris
- Cultural encounters: authentic interactions with the Datoga and Hadzabe people
- Spectacular helicopter flights over gorges, lakes, and cliffs
- Romantic drinks at sunset, bush lunches, and al fresco dinners
- Spa treatments overlooking lush landscapes

Helicopter tours through canyons and to remote locations offer incomparable adventures at Mwiba.

Legendary Expeditions – Mwiba Lodge can be found to the west of Ngorongoro Crater, in one of Tanzania's most untouched regions. Its location is spectacular, with just ten suites clustered on a rocky plateau overlooking a wild, romantic gorge, blending seamlessly into the landscape. The elegant villas offer plenty of open space and privacy, with decks framing breathtaking views across the veldt. A private rock jacuzzi and the large pool on the lodge's terrace invite leisurely relaxation, while in-suite spa treatments are also available to enjoy.

UNPARALLELED QUIET

Majestic baobab trees, river valleys meandering through the veldt, and waterholes where the reserve's wildlife congregates: The natural landscape of the private reserve surrounding the lodge is as fascinating as it is diverse. Game drives in your dedicated vehicle adapt flexibly to your family's schedule, whether by day or after dark, with experienced guides who know precisely where to go for unforgettable wildlife sightings! In the vast conservancy around Mwiba, you will seldom encounter another vehicle, experiencing rare moments of perfect tranquility in nature. This wild, untouched landscape reveals new perspectives from above. Spectacular helicopter flights soar through dramatic gorges and alight on remote rocky outcrops to enjoy drinks at sunset, an unforgettable way to experience the reserve that stretches from south of the Serengeti to Lake Eyasi. During your time at Mwiba, you also have the opportunity to discover the culture of the local tribes. Witnessing the Datoga people's rhythmic warrior dances is an electrifying experience that will stay with you forever.

Above: Suites and pool nestle against the rocky plateau high above the treetops.

Right: The lounge and its library are the perfect place for post-safari relaxation.

WHY WE LOVE IT—OUR FAMILY EXPERIENCE:

Mwiba was simply breathtaking: Our suite, or more accurately our rock villa, was perched atop a broad plateau overlooking the dramatic gorge below. We also really enjoyed the view looking out from the natural stone pool, stretching endlessly toward distant horizons. One highlight of our extraordinary lodge experience was our helicopter adventure day. Flying with open doors, we not only soared over narrow canyons but also maneuvered spectacularly through them, landing on a remote rocky outcrop for a drink—a place unreachable by any other means. The next stop was a massive boulder with a view as far as the eyes could see, after which we flew over Lake Eyasi, its mirror-smooth surface gleaming silver beneath us. The crowning moment came when the wonderful team surprised us with sunset cocktails deep in the wild—absolutely perfect with flickering torches, drinks, and that magical warm glow you can only experience in Africa.

CHEM CHEM SAFARI LODGE

The Art of Slow Safari

FAR MORE THAN GAME DRIVES AND PHOTO SAFARIS: THE FOCUS HERE IS ON TRUE IMMERSION—IN THE LANDSCAPE, THE ENCOUNTERS, AND THE RHYTHM OF NATURE. PERHAPS THE MOST INTENSIVE KIND OF SAFARI FOR FAMILIES.

Opposite page: At Chem Chem Safari Lodge, you can see giraffes, zebras, buffaloes and more without a game drive—an important animal migration corridor passes right by the lodge.

Above: Nostalgic style meets modern interior design in the tented suites.

Right: Sunset drinks with a bonfire on the shores of Lake Manyara.

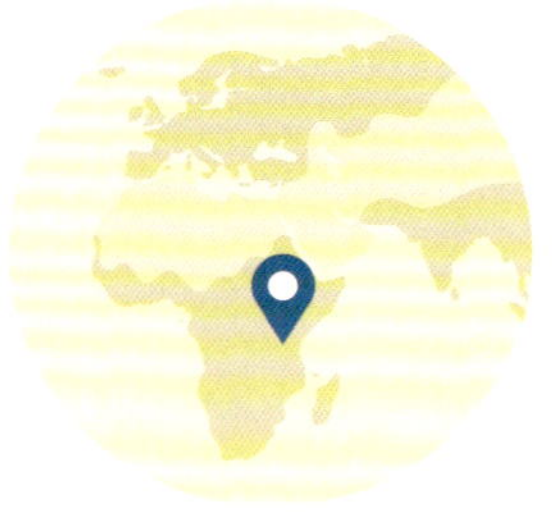

Where: In northern Tanzania between Tarangire National Park and Lake Manyara

What: 8 elegant tented suites
Vibe: Close to nature, private, highly custom, quiet and relaxed

Completely private and radiating ambiance—dinner by candlelight on the *boma* under the baobab.

Opposite page: Lions rest in the tree canopies (left), children learn fascinating insights about animal tracks from Maasai trackers (right).

Chem Chem Safari Lodge is located in northern Tanzania in a private 50,000-acre wildlife management area, marking one of the region's most vital animal migration corridors between Tarangire National Park and Lake Manyara. The lodge is a pioneer of the slow safari, emphasizing intimate experiences within your immediate environment and meaningful encounters with local people. Participating in a traditional Maasai blessing ceremony is an experience that you will treasure for a long time! The eight tented suites combine safari charm with refined elegance, each offering expansive savanna views that naturally instill calm and invite you to embrace a gentler rhythm of life. While there is no need to forgo modern amenities like the spa and fitness center, in Chem Chem, the ultimate luxury lies in watching giraffes graze from your poolside vantage point.

Chem Chem does, of course, offer game drives with a personal guide in open 4x4 vehicles, yet there's no need to board a jeep to witness wildlife up close. The most profound way to encounter the region's abundant biodiversity follows the Maasai tradition: on foot. Bush walks with expert guides reveal nature on an entirely new level, allowing even children to appreciate the rare privilege of experiencing pristine wilderness—and understand why preserving it matters so deeply.

THE UNHURRIED RHYTHM OF BUSH LIFE

At Chem Chem Safari Lodge, you live in such harmony with nature that you instinctively adopt the unhurried rhythm of bush life. Soon zebras and giraffes wander within arm's reach of your tented suite. Meals become opportunities for serenity and connection. Evenings bring guests together around the communal table, sharing the day's discoveries while the award-winning Maasai chef presents exquisite cuisine. Those seeking solitude can opt for private garden dinners, evening cocktails on Lake Manyara's shores, or an idyllic breakfast beneath gigantic baobab trees in the savanna.

HIGHLIGHTS FOR KIDS & TEENS:

- Bush walks with Maasai warriors
- Learn fascinating insights about tracking and animal behavior
- Adventure picnics and bush breakfast experiences
- Discover village life and visit local schools
- Ample time for questions and shared wonder at nature's marvels

ACTIVITIES OFFERED AT THE RESORT:

- Game drives in the private concession area and Tarangire National Park
- Guided walks through the savanna
- Get to know the culture of the Maasai community in meaningful encounters
- Safaris and romantic bush dinners in the wild
- Relaxing spa treatments, yoga, and private cocktails at sunset

WHY WE LOVE IT—OUR FAMILY EXPERIENCE:

With its slow safari philosophy, Chem Chem Safari Lodge proved the perfect fit for our family. Rather than rushing between game drives chasing the most spectacular photographs, we mindfully savored every shared moment. While classic game drives were naturally part of our experience, the focus was on the many special experiences that were allowed to unfold organically: a bush walk with a Maasai warrior, breakfast in the middle of the savanna under an ancient baobab tree, and sunset cocktails on the lakeshores as our Maasai guides lit a crackling campfire and the tranquility of the savanna gently enveloped us. During a visit to one of the nearby Maasai villages, we learned a lot about how the region's people live together and their culture—impactful, open, and very personal. Our stay at Chem Chem Safari Lodge was incredibly enriching for us as a family: exciting for the children, meaningful for us as parents—and simply wonderful together!

ANDBEYOND MNEMBA ISLAND

Discovering a Slower Place

CHARMING AND INDIVIDUAL, MNEMBA ISLAND POSSESSES A PROFOUND TRANQUILITY THAT TOUCHES THE SOUL AND LINGERS THERE. UNDERSTATED BAREFOOT LUXURY, EXCEPTIONAL SNORKELING STEPS FROM YOUR BANDA, AND HEAVENLY BEACHES YOU WILL NEVER WANT TO LEAVE ...

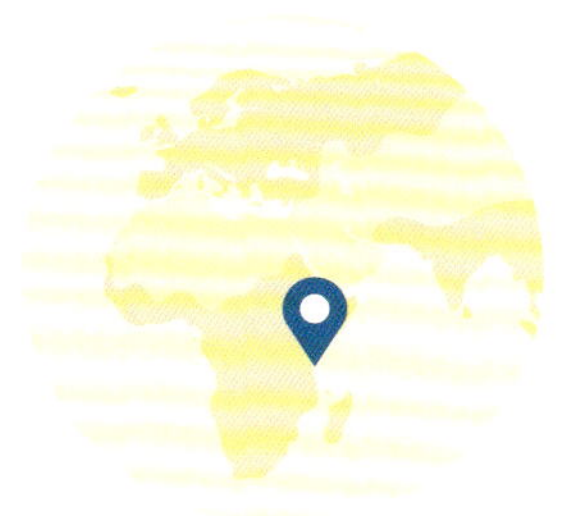

Where: On a private island off the northeast coast of Zanzibar

What: 12 bandas with direct beach access
Vibe: Slowed down, luxurious

ACTIVITIES OFFERED AT THE RESORT:

- Underwater adventures: snorkeling and diving on the reef
- On and in the water: kayaking, stand-up paddling, swimming, and sailing on a dhow
- Unwind on the beach with yoga and wellness
- Private picnics and drinks at sunset with ocean views
- Experience sustainability and conservation projects on the island

HIGHLIGHTS FOR KIDS & TEENS:

- Snorkeling adventures directly off your banda or on the reef by boat
- Dolphin watching and exploring the world of sea turtles
- Shell collecting and creative beach activities
- Plenty of space to explore and enjoy the island's barefoot freedom

Opposite page: Set out on the stand-up paddleboard into turquoise waters directly from your private banda—Mnemba is encircled by a ring of pearly white sandy beaches.

Above left: Outing to the lagoon aboard a dhow, the traditional local sailboat.

Above right: Dinner is served in a different place every day, including on the beach with your toes in the sand.

Off the coast of Zanzibar lies a veritable treasure, surrounded by pristine white sandy beaches and azure ocean waters: Mnemba Island, a tranquil, private paradise. Just twelve thatched bandas, including one for families, blend rustic architecture with inviting comfort nestled beneath the island's verdant canopy. The transition from inside to the beach outside flows seamlessly; from your covered veranda with plush lounge furnishings, you can greet each day with fresh coffee or unwind beneath the starry sky over the ocean in the evening.

DAILY SURPRISES

The true luxury of Mnemba is the silence and unhurried pace, naturally drawing you into a relaxed rhythm. Instead of rigid schedules, you will find casual barefoot luxury, along with delightful surprises like ever-changing dinner venues in hidden beach locations or secluded forest clearings. Just steps from your veranda, crystal-clear turquoise waters beckon—perfect for swimming, snorkeling, or stand-up paddleboarding. The surrounding reef, teeming with vibrant corals, sea turtles, and kaleidoscopic fish populations, also offers magnificent snorkeling. The marine biodiversity here is remarkable. Mnemba Island actively supports reef restoration through conservation initiatives while monitoring the breeding and hatching of native green sea turtles.

WHY WE LOVE IT—OUR FAMILY EXPERIENCE:

To sum it up, we have rarely felt as relaxed as we did on Mnemba Island! We enjoyed staying in the open-plan banda directly on the beach, surrounded by nature at night, listening to the sounds of the ocean and the whisper of the palm fronds. We enjoyed our first coffee in the morning snuggled up in the comfortable armchairs right in front of our accommodation, preparing us for the day's highlights: exploring the vibrant underwater world while snorkeling straight from our beach, strolling barefoot along the shoreline, then gazing at the sunset in the evening with a drink in hand before being pampered with a delicious dinner. That too was always a new experience—each evening brought a surprise location, always different, always magical, and so special! Our sunset cruise aboard a traditional dhow was truly unforgettable: sailing with the wind, gazing out over the shimmering ocean with wine in hand—one of those moments you will carry in your heart forever!

The cozy veranda flows seamlessly onto the white sandy beach—from here, the view sweeps across the endless blue ocean.

Above: Open, airy architecture featuring natural materials and lots of wood creates an inviting atmosphere.

Left: The thatched bandas blend into the island's vegetation.

Not just a place of beauty, but one of meaning

A CONVERSATION WITH ALDO MELPIGNANO, FOUNDER OF BORGO EGNAZIA.

Q: *Mr. Melpignano, what inspired you to create Borgo Egnazia, and why as a Puglian village?*
A: I didn't want to build a classic hotel complex. My vision was to create a place that feels real, like a historic Puglian village where you don't just consume culture, you live it. Puglia is my home, and I wanted to share this identity with our guests in an honest and respectful way. We built everything from the ground up, true to old traditions, with local tuff stone, handmade details, and the idea that every single bit should feel authentic. We wanted to share the essence of Puglia with others, so we worked with scenic designer Pino Brescia to design a place that is a love letter to our region, with narrow alleyways, a piazza, and houses that appear to have been standing here for centuries.

Q: *You often talk about the "Nowhere Else" concept. What does that mean?*
A: It means that what you experience here truly cannot be experienced anywhere else. Not in Rome, not in Paris, not in another luxury hotel, only here in Puglia. It is a deep emotional connection to this unique place, where our guests experience our local culture and the people who live here, with all their traditions, in a way that is unlike anywhere else in the world. We want to offer the warmth and hospitality of a private home, for guests to feel what it is like to be part of life in a southern Italian village. Our philosophy is that authenticity is the true luxury of our time. Our guests breathe in the spirit of Puglia everywhere, from the rooms to the festivals on the piazza.

"I want our guests to feel like they are staying with friends, not like they are staying at a conventional hotel."

Q: *Borgo Egnazia is also a place for family celebrations and multi-generational travel. Why is community so important here?*

"True luxury today means being moved, not impressed."

A: Because we believe that true luxury lies in spending time together, as families, as friends, as a community across generations. That is why we offer large villas, a central piazza, and village festivals that include everyone from toddlers to grandparents. I grew up surrounded by this Puglian warmth, and I want to pass it on. Many of our guests celebrate their most special moments here: weddings, birthdays, anniversaries, and they do so with the feeling of belonging to a community.

Q: *Many of your staff come from the region. What role does this local connection play?*
A: A very central one. Our staff are not just hosts; they are the soul of this place. They share their stories, their language, their warmth. Guests often tell me they form genuine connections here; sometimes developing lifelong friendships. Families are even invited into the homes of our staff for dinner. Our hotels are run by people who put their whole hearts into their work, and our guests can feel that.

"Happy staff make happy guests—that is why our team is the heart of Borgo Egnazia."

Q: *You talk about emotional luxury. What does that mean to you?*
A: Luxury has changed. It is no longer about opulence or status symbols; it is about meaning. It is about feeling seen. Being touched. Having time. Emotional quality over showy extravagance. Sometimes, a loaf of freshly baked bread, made with love by a local *massaia*, is more valuable than a designer chair. Like traditional Puglian women from the countryside, these housekeepers devote themselves to ensuring every detail in the villa is perfect, so our guests can truly settle into the slow rhythm of our way of life. The new definition of luxury is no longer clad in marble; it is simple, genuine, with heart and soul.

Q: *What roles do well-being and sustainability play at Borgo Egnazia?*
A: They are closely intertwined. Our award-winning Vair Spa draws on Puglian healing traditions and responds to each individual's needs. From the very beginning, building with local materials, involving regional producers, and respecting our environment were important to us. Here, sustainability means thinking long-term—for our guests, our community, and for Puglia itself. A place like Borgo Egnazia should not only enchant its guests today; it should also give something back to future generations.

Aldo Melpignano: "Cookie-cutter hotels are a thing of the past. People want to understand where they are—and authenticity is the key."

BORGO EGNAZIA

Experience the Essence of Puglia

LIMESTONE, CYPRESSES, THE SCENT OF LAVENDER, AND ELEGANT RESTRAINT CHARACTERIZE THE AMBIANCE AT BORGO EGNAZIA. THE RURAL CHARACTER INVITES THE WHOLE FAMILY TO SOAK UP PUGLIA'S TYPICAL ATMOSPHERE, BRIMMING WITH VITALITY.

Opposite page: Each villa has its own pool with a gorgeous Mediterranean look.

Above and right: The design is a tribute to the architectural style of Puglia, from the materials to the central piazza.

Where: Between Bari and Brindisi on the Puglian coast in southern Italy, with expansive views out over the Adriatic Sea

What: A spacious ensemble of villas, houses, and rooms
Vibe: Mediterranean flair, perfectly orchestrated, but truly charming

A synthesis of classic materials and modern design: The interior style of Borgo Egnazia is cool and elegant.

Opposite page: From the balconies and terraces of the hillside villas, guests can gaze across their private pools to the expansive landscape beyond (left). In the evenings, life comes alive with music, dancing, live cooking and entertainment (right).

"It takes a village to raise a child," as the saying goes. At Borgo Egnazia, you find yourself in just such a place—one that brings true happiness to children and their parents alike while on vacation.

Nestled among ancient olive groves high above the picturesque Adriatic coast, the authentic charm of a Puglian village is revealed at every turn. Winding lanes and hidden courtyards weave between small houses, villas with private pools, and central buildings home to restaurants and a spa. The unifying thread is a harmonious blend of traditional rural elements and thoughtful modern design—rustic and romantic, always light-filled and distinct.

EXPERIENCE AUTHENTIC PUGLIA

Borgo Egnazia comes alive through its deep connection with the surrounding landscape. Puglia's rich culture is ever-present, engaging all your senses. Hop on the bicycles provided at each villa and let freedom and wanderlust begin as you ride across the nearby golf course to the beach, along the picturesque rocky coastline. Excursions offer diverse experiences for the whole family, including rides in vintage cars, picnics at an old masseria—a typical Puglian farmhouse—and, of course, outings to discover the old town of Monopoli or the fairytale trulli village of Alberobello.

Water fun awaits at the beach club or in the large outdoor and indoor pools. The latter is part of the elegant spa, where parents can unwind while children choose between three clubs, each offering age-appropriate activities from toddlers to teenagers. In Borgo Egnazia's many restaurants—as it can only be in Italy—culinary delights reach the highest levels: Tradition and artistry go hand in hand, and there is even a dedicated restaurant just for children.

HIGHLIGHTS FOR KIDS & TEENS:

- Ample space for exploration and play
- Dedicated kids' clubs for toddlers to teens, with activities from pottery to theater
- Bike tours, beach days and excursions tailored to children
- Pizza baking, ice cream tasting and picture-perfect summer celebrations

ACTIVITIES OFFERED AT THE RESORT:

- Cycling through olive groves or to the resort's private beach
- Golf on the neighboring 18-hole course
- Sound therapy and massages in the elegant spa
- Culinary experiences: cooking workshops, olive oil tastings, and private picnics

WHY WE LOVE IT—OUR FAMILY EXPERIENCE:

Borgo Egnazia felt as if it had been created especially for celebrating life as a family. Everywhere we turned, there was a sense of joie de vivre infused with Puglian warmth. Narrow alleyways and idyllic squares invited children to play while adults enjoyed the evening over a glass of wine. Everything here is family-friendly, from the kids' clubs to the impeccable service. Our mornings began with Italian hospitality at its finest: breakfast lovingly prepared in our villa by a caring massaia. It was delicious, heartfelt, and full of warmth—a more perfect start to the day would be hard to imagine. For us, Borgo Egnazia was a unique, life-affirming place, where you join in the dancing, embracing life, feeling at home from the very first moment. We spent evenings at the festa on the square with entertainers, music, dancing, and regional specialties turning each night into a celebration of summer and of life itself—brimming with authenticity, lightness, and sheer joy.

DOMAINE DE MURTOLI

Beyond Time and Space

PRISTINE, WILD, AND BREATHTAKINGLY BEAUTIFUL—THE LANDSCAPE OF SOUTHERN CORSICA UNFOLDS IN ALL ITS SPLENDOR HERE, WHERE A VISIONARY RESORT AMONG ANCIENT SHEPHERDS' DWELLINGS TRANSFORMS SECLUSION INTO THE ART OF REFINED LUXURY.

Where: In the south of the French island of Corsica, just over half an hou-'s drive from Bonifacio

What: 20 villas and cottages scattered across extensive grounds
Vibe: Authentic, at one with nature, unique

In southern Corsica, between the mountains, the sea, and the wild and enchanting maquis, lies an extraordinary refuge: Domaine de Murtoli. Here you enter an entirely different world—untouched oak forests, olive groves, and meadows where time seems to move at its own serene pace, nature is allowed to remain as untamed as it has always been, and old traditions are deeply valued. Alongside the hotel with its elegant suites, a generous 6200-acre estate has given rise to a collection of 20 villas, all converted from historic shepherds' cottages and each lovingly designed with individual character and respect for tradition. Open fireplaces, original stone walls, and weathered wooden beams blend seamlessly with modern comforts, including private pools that appear carved from the rocks, yet even boast heating.

In addition to a spa and a beautiful secluded beach accessible only from the sea, Domaine de Murtoli even has its own 12-hole golf course, yet at this magical place that feels like another world, nothing is surprising. Experiences here abound for all ages, always in harmony with nature: horseback riding lessons, guided hikes with botanists and archaeologists, and hands-on cooking sessions using ingredients produced at the Domaine—everything feels authentic, infused with genuine passion for the respective craft.

WHEN PLEASURE BECOMES AN EXPERIENCE

What makes Domaine de Murtoli truly unique is that it is an active working farm. Cattle, pastures, olive groves, and vegetable gardens, all of which might serve as a picturesque backdrop elsewhere, supply the estate's three restaurants. The high-quality local ingredients form the basis of Corsican cuisine elevated to gourmet levels. Each culinary setting transforms dining into an experience: fine dining in the restored farmhouse, candlelight dinners in a grotto, intimate tables perched on rocky slopes with sweeping views, or a beachside meal on rustic driftwood furniture—fresh fish paired with wines from the estate's own terroir. Everything here tastes of freedom and adventure!

HIGHLIGHTS FOR KIDS & TEENS:

- Exploring meadows, streams, and beaches on discovery tours
- Guided horseback rides, herb-foraging hikes, and wildlife spotting
- Swimming in your private pool, in the river, or at a secluded, pristine sandy beach
- Cooking experiences using local ingredients, including wood-oven pizza

ACTIVITIES OFFERED AT THE RESORT:

- Horseback excursions, hikes, and boat tours along the Corsican coastline
- 12-hole golf course with unparalleled sea views
- Spa treatments in a historic stone barn and yoga in nature
- Culinary discoveries: wine and olive oil tastings, grotto dining, picnics in wild landscapes

Left: A candlelight dinner in a grotto—a truly one-of-a-kind experience!

Above: A private cove below one of the shepherds' houses with a sea view—the ultimate natural playground!

Left: Corsican delicacies with a view—the terraces of the grotto restaurant are nestled against the rock face.

Above: A laid-back lunch at the beach restaurant, where the catch of the day is served on unique driftwood tables.

WHY WE LOVE IT—OUR FAMILY EXPERIENCE:

Domaine de Murtoli fascinated us because it was so utterly different. Everywhere we went, we felt this wonderful sense of vastness, whether we were on the endless, nearly deserted beach or amid the wild, rugged beauty of the expansive estate. It always felt completely private, as if the whole place belonged to us alone. Our shepherd's villa was nestled among the rocks, close to a sheltered private cove—complete with magnificent views and excellent, discreet service. The interior was both simple and refined: heavy linen fabrics, handcrafted tableware, très français. The charm of the historic houses and the unspoiled nature carried through to the restaurants, where dining was a feast for all the senses. In the grotto restaurant, the air was filled with the aromas of wild herbs and grilled lamb, Corsican cuisine at its finest. And then, after dinner, we danced barefoot on the beach by the light of a thousand candles—a magical night that still feels like a dream. Domaine de Murtoli is one of those places that you can't shake off—you already yearn to return when you leave.

The bay with its endless sandy beach is accessible exclusively to guests of Domaine de Murtoli.

Below: The former stone shepherds' houses now offer every imaginable comfort.

Right: Even the private pools blend naturally with the architecture and surrounding landscape.

PORTO ZANTE

Big Blue Greek Paradise

HEAVENLY TRANQUILITY, COMPLETE PRIVACY, FIRST-CLASS CUISINE, AND ENCHANTINGLY CHARMING SERVICE—THESE INGREDIENTS MAKE PORTO ZANTE THE PERFECT PARADISE FOR FAMILIES.

Where: On the northern coast of the Greek island of Zakynthos in the Ionian Sea

What: Villa with private pools in lovingly landscaped gardens
Vibe: Exclusive and private, quiet and elegant

It is said that the sea is nowhere as blue as around the Greek island of Zakynthos—and anyone looking out from Porto Zante understands exactly what that means. It seems as if the colors in this part of the Mediterranean, stretching from Italy's "boot" to the Greek mainland, shine a little more intensely than anywhere else. This paradise retreat feels like a well-guarded secret.
There are only a handful of enchanting villas, each with its own private garden and pool, nestled in exclusive seclusion against the rocky coastline. Each villa is spacious and elegantly appointed, with refined Greek touches and the utmost comfort. The sandy beach lies just steps away: perfect for families with children to splash and snorkel in the sea, explore the bay by stand-up paddleboard, kayak, or pedal catamaran, or simply savor the tranquility.

COMPLETE PRIVACY, PERSONALIZED ENJOYMENT

Privacy defines this resort: intimately nestled villas, a sheltered bay with exclusive access, and exceptional personal service that makes the amenities of this world-class boutique resort feel effortlessly natural. Guests who prefer not to visit the elegant spa overlooking the sea can enjoy treatments in the comfort of their own accommodations. The same flexibility applies to the culinary creations served in two gourmet restaurants. From authentic Greek to refined Japanese cuisine, you can dine whenever and wherever you choose—on the beach, in your villa, or in your private garden, with child-friendly menus always a given. The family kids' club offers both variety and personalized attention: creative activities throughout the resort, excursions to Turtle Island, visits to the neighboring water park, or pony riding—always accompanied by affectionate, warm childcare staff.

Marvelously blue—the picturesque Shipwreck Beach.

Previous page: Even after sunset, the dramatic play of colors over the sea remains captivating.

Below left: The charming sandy bay just below the villas is intimate, perfect for families with children.

Below right: Natural stone and vibrant colors shape Porto Zante's outdoor spaces.

HIGHLIGHTS FOR KIDS & TEENS:

- Perfectly family-friendly: private pool, sheltered sandy cove, and safe sea access
- Personalized childcare and bespoke family programs
- A variety of children's activities indoors and out, from creative workshops to pony riding
- Water adventures including turtle and dolphin watching, snorkeling, kayaking, and more

ACTIVITIES OFFERED AT THE RESORT:

- Water sports and fitness: kayaking, stand-up paddle-boarding, snorkeling, private boat trips, yoga, and more
- Yacht excursions to the famous Blue Caves, Shipwreck Beach, Turtle Island, Ancient Olympia, and nearby islands
- Spa treatments in your villa or at the open-air pavilion
- Michelin-starred dining in two gourmet restaurants or private villa meals
- Wine tastings, family picnics, and cultural discovery tours

WHY WE LOVE IT—OUR FAMILY EXPERIENCE:

Porto Zante was, for us, the epitome of true private happiness: spacious villas, a sheltered location, our own pool, and a sandy, exquisite beach designed especially for children. There was no hustle and bustle, just us and the sound of the waves. The yacht excursion to Shipwreck Beach, early in the morning, allowed us to experience the deep-blue bay with crystal-clear water all to ourselves—unforgettable! Most valuable of all was the attentive yet unobtrusive service, so genuinely warm and caring that it was easy to forget we were "just" guests.

DISTINCTION MEETS GRANDEUR: AMANZOE COMBINES THE AESTHETICS OF ANCIENT ARCHITECTURE WITH LUXURIOUS MINIMALISM—A TEMPLE OF TRANQUILITY IN THE PELOPONNESIAN HILLS WHERE THE GODS THEMSELVES WOULD VACATION.

Where: Above the hills near Porto Heli on the eastern Peloponnese peninsula; about 110 miles from Athens by car

What: Around 40 pavilions and 13 villas on the hillside plateau or directly on the beach
Vibe: Minimalist elegance, tranquil, and completely private

In ancient times, the heart of Greek culture began to beat on the Peloponnese—and today, on the east coast near Porto Heli, there sits the Amanzoe Resort like a lofty temple atop the hills. Surrounded by lavender, olive trees, and cypresses, the resort's unambiguous architecture evokes a modern Acropolis: colonnaded walkways with slender columns, a harmonious blend of wood and marble, light-flooded, lofty rooms—all radiating an atmosphere of calm and lightness. Clustered around the hillside plateau, the spacious villas and pavilions offer ample privacy, each featuring a private pool. Additional pavilions can be found at the beach club, just a quick trip from the main resort by shuttle or mountain bike. Here, guests feel like they are living among the Greek gods, indulging in freshly grilled fish at the lounge and restaurant, relaxing by one of the four swimming pools—two of them designed especially for children—or enjoying activities in the sheltered bay that opens from the resort's private beach. The shimmering blue waters invite you to explore by snorkeling or stand-up paddleboarding. Children are lovingly and creatively attended to at the beach club. For those wishing to explore ancient sites such as Mycenae, Epidaurus, or Nafplio, Amanzoe offers the perfect starting point.

THE LUXURY OF RELAXED INDULGENCE

Visitors are pampered with a variety of treatments at the beach spa and the expansive Greek spa located atop the hill. The feeling of lightness continues in the resort's restaurants, where Greek culinary traditions given a top-class, modern reinterpretation.

AMANZOE

The Mount Olympus of Luxury

Previous pages: Elegant pools provide the finishing touch to the resort's architecture. Amanzoe boasts a heavenly location with stunning 360-degree views from the hills overlooking the Aegean Sea—perfect for panoramic sunsets.

Below: Relaxed dining on the beach (left) or cooling off in the pool (right)—Amanzoe offers complete freedom.

ACTIVITIES OFFERED AT THE RESORT:

- Sports and spa: water sports, tennis, yoga, fitness, and personal training
- Cycling tours, outings to hidden coves and nearby islands
- Visit ancient sites: Epidaurus, Mycenae, Nafplio, and more
- Regional culinary experiences: wine tastings, cooking classes

HIGHLIGHTS FOR KIDS & TEENS:

- Childcare at the beach club: creativity, nature and Greek cultural experiences
- Boat excursions, nature adventures, family picnics in the olive groves
- Child-friendly menus, ample space for playing, splashing, and exploring
- Villas with complete privacy, ideal for families with young children

WHY WE LOVE IT—OUR FAMILY EXPERIENCE:

Everything about Amanzoe is as impressive as it is meticulously designed—the clear architecture, the villa aesthetics, and even the cuisine: Mediterranean lightness, Greek elegance, and Asian refinement. The atmosphere breathes calm and relaxation while being exceptionally child-friendly—from the affectionate childcare at the beach club to the soothing privacy of the pavilions. Every time our gaze drifted over the olive groves and gentle hills toward the blue sea, we knew this powerful place would remain a cherished memory.

Whether dining under the pergola (above) or in the shade of gnarled olive trees (left), the resort's restaurants delight guests with both their exquisite cuisine and enchanting ambiance.

SCHLOSS ELMAU

An Alpine Jewel of Cultural Delights

THE WETTERSTEIN MOUNTAINS PROVIDE THE BACKDROP FOR A TRULY EXCEPTIONAL RESORT: AT SCHLOSS ELMAU, BOTH CHILDREN AND ADULTS CONTINUALLY DISCOVER NEW EXPERIENCES IN MUSIC, LITERATURE, WELLNESS, AND CUISINE.

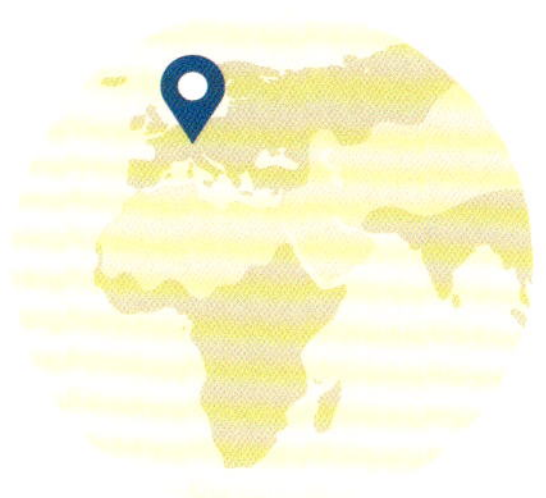

Where: In southern Germany, at the foot of the Wetterstein Mountains in the Bavarian Alps, between Mittenwald and Garmisch-Partenkirchen

What: Around 150 suites and apartments in the Hideaway and Retreat
Vibe: Elegant and refined, open and inspiring

Schloss Elmau is more than a luxurious resort in a historic setting. It is a captivating, indulgent symphony composed of extraordinary nature and cultural experiences. Guests stay in spacious suites, whether in the time-honored atmosphere of the Hideaway or in the modern Retreat building, all boasting panoramic views of the magnificent landscape. Equally as impressive as the majestic Wetterstein Mountains is Schloss Elmau's devotion to inspiring experiences. For over a century, art and culture have been at the heart of this traditional retreat. Top-class concerts, literary evenings, and thought-provoking discussions have long made it a magnet for the international cultural scene.

What awaits younger guests is just as remarkable and diverse. From toddlers to teenagers, children can mindfully explore flora and fauna, join soccer workshops led by top coaches from German Bundesliga clubs, or join in a creative cultural program that captivates even teenagers, ranging from chess and photography to technology, music, literature, and theater. Schloss Elmau proves to be every bit as open, vibrant, and diverse for its youngest visitors as for its adult guests.

ENJOYING WITH EASE

Time spent here should also be devoted to the great outdoors, as the mountain landscape remains enchanting in every season. Swim in crystal-clear alpine lakes, go horseback riding, play tennis, climb, or explore trails on mountain bikes in the summer. In the winter, the landscape transforms into a white wonderland perfect for cross-country skiing and snowshoeing through pristine snow.

Families can unwind together in dedicated spa areas, while parents seeking tranquility find serene, adults-only zones. Culinary pleasures complete the experience: Japanese–French haute cuisine in the Michelin-starred restaurant, Alpine specialties in the family restaurant, and Mediterranean cuisine at the Retreat.

Below: In the winter, the mountain world beckons with wonderful snowshoe hikes (left). The bookstore at the Hideaway has a top-quality selection available (right).

Bottom: Panoramic view of the Wetterstein Mountains from the Retreat's Shantigiri Spa.

Opposite page, left and right: The program for children and teenagers is varied, from chess games to exp oring the surrounding mountain streams.

ACTIVITIES OFFERED AT THE RESORT:

- Outdoor sports ranging from mountain biking and climbing to tennis and archery
- Winter sports, including alpine and snowshoe hiking, cross-country skiing, and more
- Yoga and dance retreats, alongside top concerts, readings, and talks
- Cultural excursions to nearby destinations such as Mittenwald, Garmisch-Partenkirchen, and Munich

HIGHLIGHTS FOR KIDS & TEENS:

- Playful learning: chess, building robots
- Cultural discovery: theater, literature, philosophy, and classical music
- Workshops for diverse interests from photography to soccer
- Emphasis on free play over structured entertainment: nature experiences, sports, campfires, and more

WHY WE LOVE IT—OUR FAMILY EXPERIENCE:

For us, Schloss Elmau is a place where thinking, experiencing, and relaxing come together. A quiet retreat for adults, a children's program that is unparalleled throughout Europe, all surrounded by nature that is absolutely stunning in every season: crystal-clear lakes and the fresh green of the mountain forests in summer, the magical white tranquility in winter. We found even rainy days here unexpectedly enjoyable: pools, libraries, fine dining experiences—Elmau has become a sanctuary of well-being for our whole family!

BACHMAIR WEISSACH

Four Seasons Among Lake and Mountains

RELAXATION OR AN ACTION-PACKED AGENDA? AS A TRADITIONAL HOTEL WITH A MODERN TWIST, BACHMAIR WEISSACH PERFECTLY BALANCES OPPOSITES—AND ITS CAREFULLY CONCEIVED FAMILY CONCEPT MAKES IT A FAVORITE PLACE FOR ALL AGES ALL YEAR ROUND.

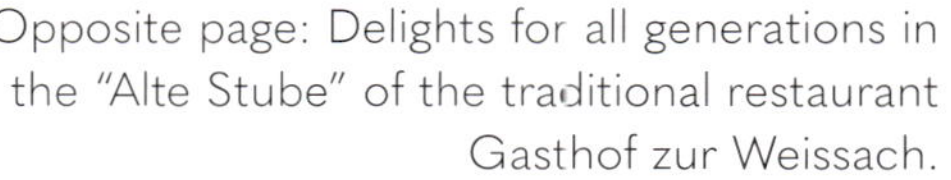

Opposite page: Delights for all generations in the "Alte Stube" of the traditional restaurant Gasthof zur Weissach.

Above: From the heated saltwater pool, the view sweeps across the stream to the magnificent mountain panorama, the autumn sun bathing everything in warm colors.

Where: In southern Germany on Lake Tegernsee in Rottach-Egern, in the heart of the Bavarian Alps

What: 140+ rooms and suites
Vibe: Traditional and cozy, stylish and elegant, exceptionally family-friendly

The stylishly appointed bistro in the Mizu Onsen Spa completes the unique wellness experience.

Opposite page, right and left: The hotel's indoor adventure world delights children and teenagers alike, offering climbing with a view, virtual experiences, and plenty of space to play and romp around!

Winter deep in snow? The mild air of spring, radiant summer days, or the interplay of autumn colors between mountains and lake? Perhaps the only question left unanswered at Bachmair Weissach is which time of year is the most beautiful to spend wonderful days there with the whole family. South of Lake Tegernsee, in Rottach-Egern, the spacious resort is clustered around a stream. What began two centuries ago as a mill inn has become a stylish retreat in the heart of the Bavarian Alps, where the cultivation of traditional Tegernsee style meets all the comfort you could desire and contemporary design. Bachmair Weissach masterfully blends the traditional with the innovative in its culinary offerings. Guests at the resort can choose from Bavarian inn classics, Italian specialties, rustic winter fondue, and an outstanding sushi bar, plus several partner restaurants in the region, guaranteeing outstanding culinary variety for every taste!

SPA, SPORTS, AND PLAYTIME

The resort's devotion to families is evident in its outstanding facilities for children and teenagers. Alongside the Japanese-inspired onsen spa, there is a dedicated family spa with pools, a bio-sauna, and a cozy lounge area. The children's club offers countless indoor and outdoor activities, while horse lovers will find what they are looking for at the riding stables. Between the mountains and the lake, winter and water sports abound, complemented by family hikes and even alpaca tours.

The resort's absolute highlight, however, is the indoor play world: a movie theater, climbing walls, slides, trampolines, a virtual reality zone, bowling lanes, a science center, and much more inspire kids of all ages, from the youngest to teenagers, so that even rainy days become a reason to celebrate!

HIGHLIGHTS FOR KIDS & TEENS:

- Extraordinary indoor adventure world with movies, slides, a climbing hall, VR worlds, and much more
- Kids' club with supervised creative and activity program
- Teen lounge, sports facilities, and activities on and around the lake
- Family spa with child-friendly pools
- Horse stables with riding lessons for all ages

ACTIVITIES OFFERED AT THE RESORT:

- Outdoor activities for every season: various winter and water sports
- Golf, tennis, biking, horseback riding, Alpine hikes, and nature walks
- Wellness in the Japanese onsen spa and in the separate family spa
- Indulgent cuisine from Bavaria to Japan, with Alpine classics, fondue, sushi, and more

WHY WE LOVE IT—OUR FAMILY EXPERIENCE:

Warm, relaxed, stylish, cozy, exciting, and relaxing all at the same time: For us, Bachmair Weissach on Lake Tegernsee is one of the most family-friendly hotels anywhere. We return as often as we can, because Tegernsee unfolds its own magic in every season: when everything is in bloom in the spring, when it is vibrant with life in the summer, glowing golden in the fall, and quietly glistening with winter snow. We love indulging in the resort's excellent sushi restaurant and unwinding together in the spa and pools. Every time we visit, our three children are especially enthusiastic about the hotel's indoor adventure world, which successfully manages to appeal to all age groups! And our dog, too, is warmly welcomed. Walks along the Weissach with our children and dog are moments of pure family joy in these beautiful natural surroundings.

Casual Thatched-Roof Luxury

ON THE EDGE OF KEITUM, A PICTURESQUE VILLAGE OF HISTORIC CAPTAINS' HOUSES ON GERMANY'S NORTHERNMOST ISLAND OF SYLT, SEVERIN'S IS A RETREAT THAT EFFORTLESSLY BLENDS SERENITY, INDULGENCE, AND NORDIC ELEGANCE WITH AUTHENTIC ISLAND SPIRIT, WARM HOSPITALITY, AND A WELCOMING ATMOSPHERE INVITING YOU TO UNWIND, BREATHE DEEPLY, AND SIMPLY BE.

Where: In the village of Keitum on the eastern side of Sylt, an island in Germany's far north

What: 62 rooms and suites, plus 22 apartments and 5 villas
Vibe: Elegant and relaxed, infused with Nordic tranquility

Left: The path to the Wadden Sea tidal flats begins just steps from the resort.

Opposite page: Severin's blends traditional Frisian thatched-roof architecture with cozy, modern flair.

SEVERIN'S
RESORT & SPA

HIGHLIGHTS FOR KIDS & TEENS:

- Nature adventures along the Wadden Sea, kite flying, pony rides, the Keitum adventure playground, and more
- Kids Club with a daily-changing program of games, creative workshops, and exploring the outdoors
- Spacious spa area with a glass-roofed pool and family sauna; swimming lessons available upon request
- Perfect for pet-loving families, as dogs are warmly welcome!

ACTIVITIES OFFERED AT THE RESORT:

- Spa featuring an indoor pool, saunas, treatments, and yoga sessions
- Family-friendly excursions, including Wadden Sea hikes, horseback riding, and cycling tours
- Seasonal highlights, such as cooking classes and evenings celebrating typical Sylt flavors

Sylt's long sandy beaches and winding dune trails are a favorite playground for children eager to explore.

Anyone traveling to Sylt looks forward to the vast horizon over the sea, the cries of seagulls, a fresh salt-tinged breeze, and charming thatched houses—exactly what awaits guests at Severin's. Situated on the edge of Keitum, a village famous for its historic captains' houses, the exclusive resort merges traditional Frisian architecture with modern, inviting design and relaxed atmosphere.

The rooms, apartments, and villas are elegantly designed with natural materials, offering understated luxury. Families will especially appreciate the maisonette suites, where children have their own cozy sleeping alcoves, and the family villas, thoughtfully designed with private kitchens, patios, or gardens. A creative program for children includes short excursions and nature experiences along the Wadden Sea tidal flats. While parents are pampered in the spa, kids are equally well cared for in the Kids Club or can even book swimming lessons. Culinary offerings focus on sophisticated regional dishes served in the resort's two restaurants.

FAMILY EXPERIENCES IN THE OUTDOORS

Guests who prefer to explore the island without the hotel's bicycles can enjoy a stroll through the picturesque village of Keitum, where boutiques and galleries occupy historic captain's houses. The Old Frisian House and the Sylt Museum are also well worth a visit. Nearby, the stunning natural landscape of heathland, dunes, salt marshes, and tidal flats unfolds—one breath of the fresh, soothing air, and you know you have truly arrived on this blissful Nordic island.

Above left: Children enjoying swimming lessons in the pool.

Above right: In the family suites, kids have their own cozy sleeping alcove.

Right: The Kids Club features a daily-changing program for the youngest guests.

WHY WE LOVE IT—OUR FAMILY EXPERIENCE:

We experienced Severin's on Sylt as a sanctuary of peace and mindful slowing down. Overlooking the Wadden Sea near Keitum, it offered our family ample space for genuine, shared moments. One of our favorite memories was the guided Wadden Sea hike—connecting with nature while playfully absorbing knowledge made it a special experience even for the youngest children. Exploring the island's vastness by bike along the dikes was another highlight, as was feeling the fresh wind in our hair on the seemingly endless, dune-fringed beaches. A smaller yet especially cherished outing took us to nearby Morsum Cliff, where we enjoyed expansive views across the Wadden Sea and fine delicacies at Severin's sister hotel, Morsum Cliff. Pure freedom—this is a piece of the North Sea you carry home in your heart. We dream of returning one day with our dog, as four-legged family members receive the same warm welcome at Severin's.

Wild and Wonderful, with the Ocean Nearby

BETWEEN THE RICE FIELDS, CORK OAKS, PINE GROVES, AND ENDLESS SANDY BEACHES OF THE ALENTEJO LIES SUBLIME COMPORTA—A PLACE OF TRANQUILITY WHERE EVERYTHING SEEMS TO MOVE TO A GENTLE RHYTHM.

Where: Near the vast beach of Comporta in the Portuguese region of Alentejo

What: 23 rooms and 22 cabana villas
Vibe: Natural boho-style chic, exclusive and secluded

True treasures are often hidden, and one such gem is found in the Alentejo region, just an hour south of Lisbon. Nestled between forests, rice fields, and pristine dunes is Sublime Comporta, one of Portugal's best-kept secrets. Integrated into its surroundings, the resort exudes a light, airy atmosphere perfect for a family vacation with plenty of comfort. Bright, spacious villas with large windows using plenty of wood and linen, are scattered amid shady pine groves. Private terraces and pools offer ideal spaces for relaxing with the whole family.
The vast grounds provide ample room for children to play and explore, while bicycles invite guests to discover the surroundings. Instead of a conventional kids' club, the resort emphasizes shared experiences such as children's yoga, cookie baking, and tennis lessons. Adults can indulge in spa and wellness treatments, while local culinary culture is brought to life through wine tastings. Portugal's cultural highlights, including the UNESCO World Heritage city of Évora and the vibrant capital Lisbon, are within easy reach.

DISCOVER THE VASTNESS BETWEEN DUNES AND BEAUTIFUL BEACHES

One of Comporta's greatest treasures is revealed where the dunes meet the sea—just minutes away is a 60-kilometer (37-mile) stretch of some of Portugal's finest white-sand beaches, bordered by the azure waters of the Atlantic. The beach offers space for everything here, whether splashing in the waves, surfing, kiteboarding, horseback riding at sunset, or simply being pampered at the resort's beach club. The resort's restaurants and bars provide exquisite culinary experiences, focusing on Alentejo specialties made from sustainably sourced local ingredients. Guests can enjoy these at the main restaurant, the organic garden restaurant, or poolside.

HIGHLIGHTS FOR KIDS & TEENS:

- Explore nature in the pine forests, dunes, and along the long sandy beaches
- Spacious villas with private pools and plenty of room for free play
- Riding lessons, bike tours, and family picnics
- Creative kids' workshops and children's menus

ACTIVITIES OFFERED IN THE REGION:

- Biking and hiking tours, horseback rides along the miles of beaches
- Kitesurfing, surfing, and beach walks
- Yoga, Pilates, massages, and treatments in the nature-inspired spa
- Wine tastings, cooking classes, and visits to traditional markets
- Outings to nearby nature reserves and cultural highlights

Left: Past the dunes lie the wide beach and the waves of the Atlantic.

Above: The most delightful way to explore the expansive resort grounds is by bicycle.

An impressive golf course ensconced in the dunes near Sublime Comporta.

WHY WE LOVE IT—OUR FAMILY EXPERIENCE:

Who would have thought Sublime Comporta would remind us so much of Sylt? The vastness of the Atlantic, the endless beach where you can walk for hours without encountering another soul, the wind tousling your hair, the sand beneath your feet—everything exuded a feeling of lightness and serenity. It was not a lively beach resort that awaited us here, but a genuine retreat immersed in pristine nature, characterized by aesthetics and tranquility. The blend of modern design and boho-style chic instantly charmed us: bright, relaxed, casual but well-conceived, sustainable and yet so stylish. Our days were simple pleasures: cycling to the beach through the scent of pine trees, savoring freshly harvested produce in the organic garden restaurant, relaxing in the breezy shade by our pool. And even without an action-packed children's club program, we always felt completely welcome at the resort with our children.

Above: The spacious cabana villas, each with a private pool, offer relaxed seclusion for the whole family.

Right: In the resort's restaurants, guests can savor authentic Alentejo cuisine.

ASHFORD CASTLE

Regal Living on the Emerald Isle

A FAIRYTALE CASTLE WITH A RICH HISTORY AND LUXURIOUS AMBIANCE IN WESTERN IRELAND: BETWEEN AFTERNOON TEA AND SPA TREATMENTS, HORSEBACK RIDING, FALCONRY, AND IRISH WOLFHOUNDS, REAL ADVENTURE AWAITS THE ENTIRE FAMILY.

Opposite page: Ashford Castle rises imposingly on the shores of Lough Corrib.

Above: Sleep like royalty in rooms furnished with stylish elegance.

Right: Fishing on the lake by boat—it doesn't get more Irish than this!

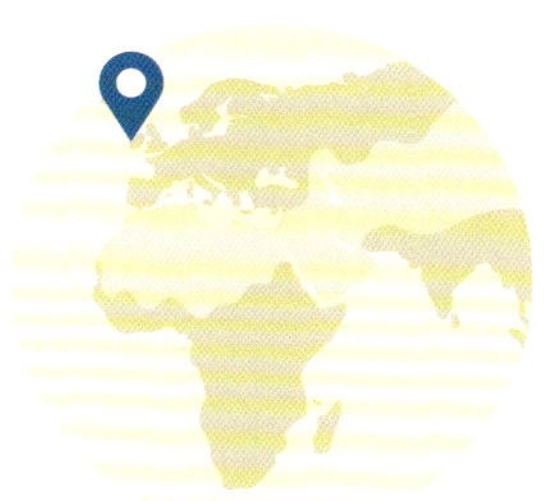

Where: In Cong, County Mayo in western Ireland, on the shores of Lough Corrib

What: 83 rooms and suites
Vibe: Stylish, elegant, and classic, historic ambiance

A unique experience: Interact with the birds of prey used in falconry.

Opposite page, right and left: Even rainy days are fun when you walk the wolfhounds in the castle park or play chess in Oak Hall under the watchful eye of Ashford's ancestors.

Where else but at Ashford Castle can you spend the night steeped in centuries of history? Deep in the west of Ireland above the shores of Lough Corrib, this 13th-century fortress fulfills childhood dreams by giving you the feeling of living like royalty in its time-honored walls. It has been restored with great attention to detail, and its exquisitely decorated rooms combine magnificent antiques with modern comforts, with open fires providing a cozy atmosphere, and windows offering breathtaking views of the picturesque lake and parklands.

The castle's restaurants and bars are lavishly opulent, with grand chandeliers, fine silverware, wood paneling, and history-rich paintings creating a majestic atmosphere to savor modern Irish cuisine. Classic afternoon tea is a charming ritual steeped in authentic Irish tea culture you will not want to miss. For wine lovers, the hidden castle vaults provide an exclusive tasting experience. Those skeptical that wellness could flourish within medieval walls need only step into the stunning glass spa in the style of a Victorian-style greenhouse overlooking the riverbank, a luxurious haven offering treatments, fitness facilities, and relaxation.

LIVING LIKE THE LANDED GENTRY OF OLD

At least as impressive as the castle itself is the surrounding landscape, offering ample space for family adventures. Exploring the castle grounds alongside the wonderfully gentle Irish wolfhounds is a delight not only enjoyed by children. Guests can immerse themselves in pursuits once enjoyed by the landed gentry—horseback riding, archery, rowing a wooden boat across the lake on a fishing trip, or visiting the falconry. At the same time, more contemporary activities abound, from golf and tennis to kayaking excursions. Ashford Castle enchants in every season, combining unique experiences with the timeless elegance of a bygone era.

ACTIVITIES OFFERED AT THE RESORT:

- Active outdoor pursuits such as horseback riding, bicycling, golf, and lake fishing
- Spa facilities with indoor pool and relaxing treatments
- Exclusive fine dining and authentic teatime experiences in a historic setting
- Wine tastings, whiskey samplings, and cozy storytelling by the fireplace
- Outings to nearby attractions including Cong Abbey, the Cliffs of Moher, and more

HIGHLIGHTS FOR KIDS & TEENS:

- Magical castle setting with its own parklands—immerse yourself in adventure and nature
- Memorable walks with the famous Irish wolfhounds
- Activities including archery, horseback riding, falconry visits, boat trips, and bicycling tours
- Quality family time with picnics in the castle park and traditional Afternoon Tea

WHY WE LOVE IT—OUR FAMILY EXPERIENCE:

Staying at Ashford Castle felt like stepping into another world and time. We lived like lords of a bygone era—surrounded by tradition and a proud sense of history. The children loved dressing up for dinner and roaming the castle's time-honored corridors, and truth be told, we adults were just as enchanted. Antique furnishings, roaring fireplaces, and the knight's armor in the foyer—so lifelike it seemed ready to spring into action—brought the past vividly to life! Ashford Castle is a dream for animal lovers, too. Strolling the grounds with the majestic Irish wolfhounds was unforgettable, and the falconry experience, feeling birds of prey alight gently on our arms, moved us deeply. Beyond the castle, the surrounding region holds its own treasures: watching a shepherd at work with his dogs or standing in awe at the dramatic Cliffs of Moher, famed as a Harry Potter filming location. We carried home the magic of Ashford Castle in our hearts.

Traveling with children means making time for wonder

RECOGNIZED BY *CONDÉ NAST TRAVELER* AS "TOP TRAVEL SPECIALIST 2024 FOR CENTRAL AMERICA," KATRIN KIRCHHOFF SPECIALIZES IN AUTHENTIC OFF-THE-BEATEN-PATH EXPERIENCES WITH CUSTOM, SLOW-PACED FAMILY TRAVEL.

Q: *Katrin, you live with your family in San José, Costa Rica. How did you end up there?*
A: Honestly, it was pure chance! I grew up in Asia and I moved to Costa Rica after finishing my studies. I've been living here for over 20 years now, and every morning when I look up at the blue sky and hear the birds singing, I feel as if I've landed in paradise. I founded Travel Pioneers with my business partner Catalina in 2017. Since we are both mothers, we especially enjoy creating trips in collaboration with The Family Project.

Q: *The diverse natural paradises of Costa Rica, Nicaragua, Panama, and Colombia still remain hidden gems. What makes them so suitable for family travel?*
A: Latin America is perfect for families because it uniquely combines adventure, nature, culture, and beautiful beaches in a very small area. Where else can you hear howler monkeys, see scarlet macaws flying overhead, and spot sloths in the trees? Active volcanoes, rainforests, and idyllic beaches can all be experienced on a single trip, including activities for all ages, from easy hikes in national parks to encounters with sea turtles, kayaking through mangroves, and ziplining through the rainforest.

Q: *Many parents long for authentic experiences but also have safety concerns. What advice would you give them?*
A: Costa Rica, Panama, and Colombia in particular have a very good tourist infrastructure in place, which gives parents peace of mind and makes planning easier. All of these countries remain wonderfully unspoiled, appealing to families who enjoy comfort yet also want to discover authentic destinations. Our team is available 24/7 during the trip, and I am personally on call in case of emergencies. Thanks to our concierge team, there is always a little surprise waiting

"Costa Rica, Panama, and Colombia have a very good tourist infrastructure in place. All of these countries are also unspoiled, appealing to families who enjoy comfort yet also want to discover authentic destinations."

Katrin Kirchhoff has called Costa Rica home for over 20 years and specializes in finding the perfect balance of adventure and safety for traveling families.

in the hotel room. We can take the safety concerns away from the families, we test everything we recommend with our own children first!

Q: *Travel Pioneers stands for individual, unhurried travel. How does slow travel change the travel experience for families?*
A: Slow travel means experiencing more mindfully and more deeply, focused on personalization. Since climate and time zone changes can be challenging for families with young children, we always recommend starting gently. Arrive, settle in, and recharge on the beach before your adventures begin. Instead of constantly changing locations, it's about focusing on experiences. This leaves more time for encounters—and our local guides often become so close to the visiting families that children later send them letters and drawings. Slow travel is also more sustainable. We teach children not to consume highlights one after another, but to discover new environments respectfully and appreciatively. Some moments from our own travels remain unforgettable. In the El Viejo Wetlands, we experienced the beautiful blend of tradition, culture, and agriculture, preparing tortillas together dressed in traditional garb. On the Osa Peninsula, we showed the children whales in the Golfo Dulce and even encountered a puma at the lodge—absolutely magical! Experiences like this are often possible in October, considered the "rainy season," when Costa Rica is free of crowds.

"Slow travel means a more mindful, more intense experience. We always recommend starting gently. Arrive, settle in, and recharge on the beach before your adventures begin."

Q: *Which destinations do you recommend for truly experiencing the lifestyle of the region? And which are closest to your own heart?*
A: There is so much to discover! It's important to take the time to relax and enjoy the wonderful hotels while also exploring what makes each region unique. From San José we can reach active volcanoes—it's fascinating to walk right up to the crater! Depending on the season, from July to October in Tortuguero we can watch turtles laying their eggs or even witness them hatching. Adventure is guaranteed with canopy tours through the jungle, abseiling down waterfalls, or rafting for the adults. A particularly cool highlight is night hikes in Monteverde with scorpion hunting under UV light! Personally, I love the Osa Peninsula, one of the most authentic places in southern Costa Rica, far from mass tourism. At dawn, you wake to the calls of monkeys and birds, toucans flutter by, and in the evening the sounds of the jungle lull you to sleep. What I want families to take home from our trips are shared experiences and the thrill of discovery, whether it is watching a turtle, cooking with locals, or leaping into a jungle waterfall for the first time.

Organic Hacienda Among the Palms

THIS ECO-RESORT HAS TRULY FOUND ITS NICHE: TUCKED BETWEEN AN IDYLLIC BAY AND THE JUNGLE ALONG NICARAGUA'S COAST, IT LEADS THE WAY IN SUSTAINABLE TRAVEL.

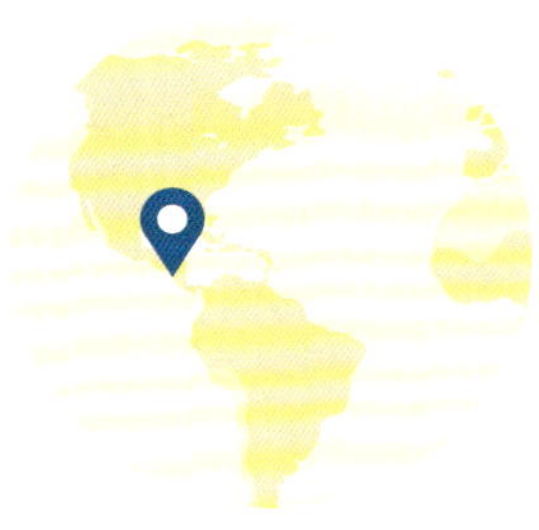

Where: On the Pacific coast in southern Nicaragua, between beach, jungle, and nature reserve

What: 15 bungalows and 3 private villas
Vibe: Close to nature and relaxed, focused on resource conservation

A sandy beach under the palm trees, a jungle camp, or a vacation on a farm? What sounds like polar opposites in family vacation planning comes together harmoniously at Morgan's Rock eco-resort on Nicaragua's nearly untouched Pacific coast. Set within a 3,700-acre nature reserve, the villas and most bungalows feature private pools for cooling off and breezy verandas, with architecture that is open and relaxed. Built eco-consciously with abundant wood and natural materials and integrated into the jungle, these dwellings practically blend into nature while simultaneously offering stunning views of the private bay.

Down on the sandy beach, guests can choose between action or relaxation. Anyone wanting action can ride the waves on a boogie board, take surfing lessons, paddle out on a stand-up paddleboard or kayak, or ride the beautiful horses. And if you just want to unwind, enjoy the view of the water from a hammock at the beach hut. Late afternoon is the perfect time for a hike up the nearby hill, atop which a spectacular panorama unfolds at sunset. Guided day or night nature expeditions lead families in search of adorable capuchin monkeys and sloths, captivating explorers of all ages.

SUSTAINABILITY EXPERIENCED FIRSTHAND

Depending on the season, guests can witness turtle hatchlings making their first journey to the ocean, an experience that teaches children the importance of preserving the natural world, a fundamental value embraced and lived by Morgan's Rock private reserve. Sustainability guides every action here, from resource-conserving construction to ecosystem protection and the biodynamic farm that supplies the resort. Children love lending a hand at the hacienda, and when the friendly chef turns the freshly gathered eggs into a delicious breakfast omelet, it tastes twice as good!

HIGHLIGHTS FOR KIDS & TEENS:

- Immerse yourself in farm life: milk the cows, gather eggs, feed the animals
- Horseback riding on the beach and through the jungle
- Surfing lessons and bodyboarding, paddleboarding in the bay, kayaking through the mangroves
- Witness baby turtles hatching, depending on the season
- Go on expeditions to spot monkeys and sloths

ACTIVITIES OFFERED AT THE RESORT:

- Hiking and wildlife watching in the nature reserve
- Yoga with views over the treetops
- Farm-to-table cooking classes
- Sunset hike to the lookout point
- Cultural outings in the surrounding area

Above: Farm-to-table right from the start—children can gather the eggs from the chickens, which are then used to prepare breakfast.

Left: Riding through the bay on horseback is simply amazing!

Below: The veranda outside the bungalow is the perfect spot for an afternoon siesta.

Opposite page, top left: Idyllic beach beneath the palms, with plenty of space for children to play and explore.

Opposite page, top right and bottom: The cabana-style restaurant and bar surround the expansive main pool.

WHY WE LOVE IT—OUR FAMILY EXPERIENCE:

Morgan's Rock made it easy for us to experience pure nature. Endless beaches, lush greenery, and mysterious jungle paths winding between towering trees and tangled vines—with every step, we could feel life moving here at a slower, gentler, and more authentic pace. We have seldom slept as well and as restfully as we did in our cozy bungalow nestled in the jungle, surrounded by the sounds of nature. The rustling of the wind in the trees, the morning calls of howler monkeys, the chirping of crickets at night—all of this wove together into a natural symphony that lulled us into deeper, more peaceful slumber than anywhere else. Visiting the resort's hacienda was a true highlight. Our children had tremendous fun milking the cows, gathering eggs in the barn, and helping feed the animals. Everything felt so simple, honest, and was done with such devotion, including the lovingly prepared farm breakfast made with the freshly gathered eggs! A genuine haven of well-being, with genuine warmth and an almost meditative serenity that stayed with us long after we left.

ORIGINS LUXURY LODGES

Up in the Clouds

SET AMID THE JUNGLE OF COSTA RICA'S VOLCANIC HIGHLANDS, THIS HIDDEN PARADISE IS PERFECT FOR ANYONE SEEKING WILDERNESS, STRIKING ARCHITECTURE, AND OUTSTANDING CULINARY ARTISTRY.

Opposite page: Nestled in the highland jungle, Villa Vertigo offers absolute seclusion and magnificent views.

Above: The veranda of Origins Floral's restaurant appears to float above the treetops.

Right: Children can join guided night walks, and, with a little luck, catch a glimpse of the elusive red-eyed tree frog.

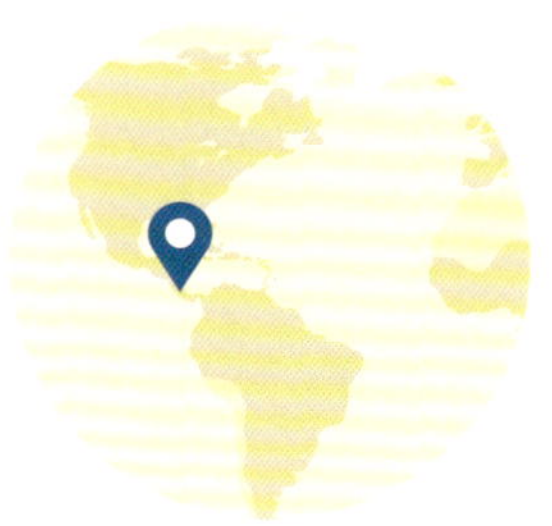

Where: In northern Costa Rica near the Nicaraguan border, about 85 miles northwest of San José as the crow flies

What: 7 lodges on stilts and 7 villas nestled in the greenery
Vibe: Design merges with jungle, exclusive and very private

In seventh heaven—from the spectacular infinity pool at Origins Floral, the view sweeps across the endless horizon.

Opposite page: A trail ride through the green hills is a great experience (left). There is always plenty to see in the trees around the casitas (right).

In the dense greenery of the rainforest between the Tenorio and Miravalles volcanoes in northern Costa Rica, the villas of Origins Astral offer families and groups of friends generous space and breathtaking views. From the stilted lodges of Origins Floral, families with older children enjoy the magnificent panoramic views above the treetops. The highlight here: private plunge pools heated by wood-burning stoves. The main houses of both lodges are architectural masterpieces. Beneath the striking grass-covered roof of Floral, guests can spend entire days in the open living area simply reading or gazing into the distance. The curved infinity pool is spectacular—you feel as if you are swimming straight into the sky. In the futuristically designed Astral, with its 80-foot lagoon and private pools, provides an inviting haven for families. On the culinary front, the Origins Luxury Lodges set new standards with their gourmet cuisine. Many ingredients come from their own gardens and are fermented, refined, and lovingly prepared by the creative kitchen team. There is a children's menu as well, ensuring both young and adult guests' palates are equally satisfied. Those who wish to can even cook alongside the chefs and explore the diversity of Costa Rican cuisine themselves.

PLENTY OF ACTIVITIES FOR LITTLE EXPLORERS

On exciting walks with nature guides, explorers of all ages can experience the incredible biodiversity around Origins, from medicinal plants to the approximately 150 bird species native to the area. Especially recommended are the tours after nightfall, where guests track nocturnal animals and experience the fascination of bioluminescent fungi species. Action-packed adventures await on the nearby rivers, with waterfall hikes, whitewater rafting for the grown-ups, and floating tours that are great fun for younger children.

HIGHLIGHTS FOR KIDS & TEENS:

- Drift along the river on floating tours, suitable for children roughly five and older
- Guided nature walks, including night tours with fascinating wildlife viewing
- Explore nearby waterfalls and natural hot springs
- Go bouldering and enjoy free play around the lodge
- Family excursions in the region: chocolate tours, zip-lining, hanging bridges, and more
- Children's club with creative workshops, including pottery, birdhouse building, candle making, and beekeeping

ACTIVITIES OFFERED AT THE RESORT:

- Guided hikes through the jungle
- Out and about on land and water: horseback riding, rafting, and floating on the river
- Birdwatching and animal spotting
- Discover Costa Rica's culinary delights in cooking classes and chocolate workshops
- Yoga on a spectacular platform between the treetops with stunning views

WHY WE LOVE IT – OUR FAMILY EXPERIENCE:

The Origins Luxury Lodge impressed us more than almost any other place in Costa Rica. It is a destination we are eager to return to, because it brings together everything we love: nature and design, tranquility and adventure. From the casitas, the endless view stretches across the forest all the way to Lake Nicaragua, surrounded by simply breathtaking scenery–wild, serene, and lushly green. The food was exceptional–creative, refined, and bursting with flavor. And then there is the extraordinary infinity pool. Standing at its elegantly curved edge, looking out over the mirrored water, you feel as if you could melt right into the sky. The horseback ride with the lovingly cared-for horses was another highlight. Our favorite ritual was slipping into the warm plunge pool before bed and again at sunrise, breathing deeply and listening to the sounds of nature, which sounded like music in our ears.

NAYARA TENTED CAMP

Rainforest Love

GLAMPING WITH VOLCANO VIEWS, HOT SPRINGS, AND RAINFOREST ADVENTURES: AT NAYARA, YOU EXPERIENCE NATURE UP CLOSE AND WITH ALL YOUR SENSES, ALL WITH A SUSTAINABLE TOUCH.

Where: In the north of Costa Rica, between the Arenal volcano and the eponymous river

What: 29 luxury tents, 2 family tents, and 6 private residences
Vibe: A nature paradise

Set in the rainforest at the foot of Arenal, Costa Rica's youngest volcano, Nayara Tented Camp is a luxurious haven for travelers who want to immerse themselves in nature without sacrificing comfort. Elegant glamping suites peek through the jungle's green canopy. The entire resort is designed with sustainability and environmental compatibility in mind. The tented suites are built on stilts to minimize their impact on nature. A glimpse inside the spacious interiors with canopy beds and wooden floors ensure comfort without compromise. By the time you sink into the thermal pool on your terrace, serenaded by birdsong and gazing at the magnificent Arenal volcano, you will have fallen in love with the paradise that is Nayara.

IN AND ALONGSIDE NATURE

Nayara is the perfect place to discover Costa Rica's natural diversity. Children delight in watching the endearing sloths in the reforested conservation area surrounding the camp. Monkeys and coatis cross your path at every turn, joining you at breakfast or on your way to the spa. Little nature lovers can spot countless bird species here, from tiny hummingbirds to brightly colored toucans. More jungle adventures await behind every tree: bravely cross hanging bridges through the rainforest canopy, hike through waterfall mist, stroll across lava fields, and be sure to take a dip in the famous hot springs!

Previous pages: The luxurious grand tents offer plenty of space, ideal for families with younger children.

Opposite page: The tented suites were built on stilts for minimal impact on the environment.

Below and bottom left: There is so much to discover on the guided nature excursions, like the playful coatis leaping through the trees.

Below right: From the private thermal pool, you can enjoy a breathtaking view all the way to Arenal volcano.

HIGHLIGHTS FOR KIDS & TEENS:

- Discovery trail with adorable sloths
- Bathing in natural hot springs and picnics by the volcano
- Floating tour on the river, also suitable for small children
- Wildlife watching at the camp
- Visit to an organic cocoa plantation with a small local chocolate factory

ACTIVITIES OFFERED AT THE RESORT:

- High up in the jungle: guided hike across hanging bridges
- Volcano treks with experienced nature guides
- Rafting, horseback riding, and ziplining in the area
- Pure relaxation and well-being: spa, yoga, hot springs, and exceptional cuisine

WHY WE LOVE IT—OUR FAMILY EXPERIENCE:

We were truly amazed by how much there was to experience at Nayara Tented Camp, from a sloth discovery trail and thrilling walks across dizzying hanging bridges through the rainforest to a wonderful volcano hike, topped off with a lovingly prepared picnic at the foot of the mountain. The lodge itself instantly felt like home. Our tents with our own private thermal pool on the deck were elegant and comfortable, while inviting plenty of nature in, and the view of the volcano in the evening light was simply magical.

Pristine Island Worlds

A REFUGE OF EXCLUSIVE SECLUSION, SURROUNDED BY CRYSTAL-CLEAR OCEAN WATERS AND UNMATCHED BIODIVERSITY, LIES OFF THE COAST OF PANAMA: ISLAS SECAS IS THE DREAM DESTINATION FOR THOSE WHO CHERISH NATURE AND FREEDOM, SERENE TRANQUILITY, AND A TOUCH OF ADVENTURE AT SUNSET.

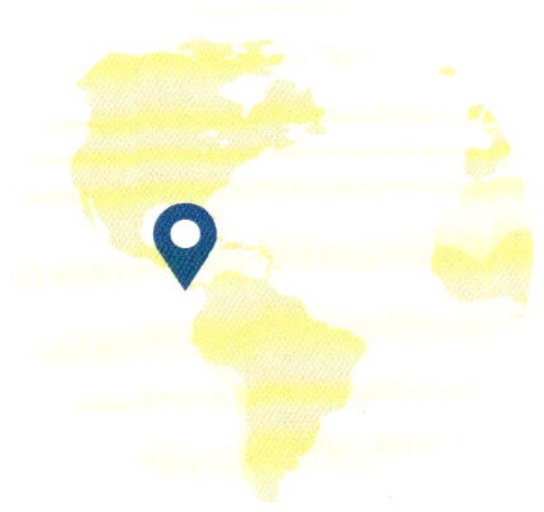

Where: In the Gulf of Chiriquí National Marine Park off the Panamanian coast

What: 7 casitas, including 3 tents, plus a spacious villa
Vibe: Sustainable, secluded

Islas Secas is not a place you stumble upon by accident. This exclusive resort lies on a private archipelago in the Gulf of Chiriquí off Panama's Pacific coast, so remote that it can only be reached by private plane. For guests, the adventure begins with the approach from the air, when the fourteen rugged volcanic islands scattered across a more than a 35,000-acre marine reserve look like lush green brushstrokes on the deep blue ocean. Thirteen of them are protected in their pristine state by the resort's foundation.

On the resort island, sustainability and harmony with nature are guiding principles. Solar power, consistent recycling, and water treatment are standard here, and the casitas were built using a minimally invasive approach and renewable materials. The resort offers just a handful of luxurious accommodations with understated architecture. Three of the casitas are tented retreats; four are built in Panamanian style, reminiscent of elegant treehouses. Some afford sweeping jungle views, while others gaze out across the vast ocean. For those seeking ultimate exclusivity, there is a magnificent villa with four suites and the ultimate luxury amenities.

BIODIVERSITY AND PHYSICAL ACTIVITY

Guests who appreciate tranquility and style combined with immersive nature experiences will find paradise here. The surrounding marine reserve is a thriving corridor of marine life, and on boat safaris, guests can spot the "Big Blue Five"– manta rays, sharks, humpback whales, whale sharks, and sea turtles. The waters offer endless possibilities: scuba diving to discover the underwater world, snorkeling along the reef, kayaking through mangroves, or gliding across the surface by stand-up paddleboard, sailboat, eFoil, or Seabob. Depending on your mood, you can explore the wild side of the islands or simply drift gently through the stillness of quiet coves.

ACTIVITIES OFFERED AT THE RESORT:

- Sports and action: diving, snorkeling, eFoiling, sport fishing, and sailing
- Outings to neighboring islands and the marine reserve
- Relaxation at its finest: yoga, spa treatments, and cocktails at sunset
- Learn about sustainability initiatives and marine conservation efforts

HIGHLIGHTS FOR KIDS & TEENS:

- Snorkeling and kayaking adventures for young explorers
- Guided nature walks and birdwatching
- Creative workshops and family pizza-making sessions
- Boat excursions with dolphin spotting

Top: Relaxing by the beautiful infinity pool.

Above: More than 100 bird species and around 130 plant species call Islas Secas home. Family-friendly trails through the jungle invite you to explore on guided nature walks.

Left: Teens and adults alike will delight in beach days on the archipelago.

The first sailing experience on a Hobie catamaran is fun right from the start.

The infinity pool seems to merge seamlessly with the ocean as your gaze drifts toward the horizon.

WHY WE LOVE IT—OUR FAMILY EXPERIENCE:

Even the journey itself to Islas Secas felt like an adventure—flying in a private plane over the Panama Canal, the view from the window was absolutely breathtaking, truly wowing us. The moment we landed, the feeling of discovering something extraordinary was confirmed. It was remote, cool, and simply paradise. The villas are stylish, the tented suites laid-back yet elegant: We were lucky to experience both of these, and immediately felt at home in each. The nature within the biodiverse marine reserve was spectacular, and the range of sports activities was as varied as the surroundings. We hardly knew what to try first: sailing, diving, eFoiling, kayaking, ... everything our hearts desired! What completely won us over, though, was the food. Every meal was exquisite, pure gourmet pleasure, but our personal highlight? The heavenly desserts the pâtissier created for us at each lunch and dinner!

Above: The restaurant under the palm trees serves freshly caught delicacies Panama-style.

Right: Gorgeous bays beckon with turquoise blue water and beautiful beaches.

The Truly Wild West

SPECTACULARLY LOCATED IN THE RICHLY FORESTED, FJORD-LIKE LANDSCAPE OF VANCOUVER ISLAND, THIS LODGE OFFERS A UNIQUE GLAMPING EXPERIENCE: NATURE OUTINGS ARE PERFECTLY PAIRED WITH LUXURY AND COMFORT.

Where: On the inner shores of a sound on Vancouver Island off the Pacific coast of Canada

What: 25 spacious glamping tents
Vibe: Far away from it all, rustic yet exclusive

Left: From the "Ivanhoe deck", guests can enjoy sweeping views of Clayoquot Sound, ideally with a drink in hand.

Opposite page, top left and right: Wooden walkways wind through the forest, connecting glamping tents that embody stylish minimalism.

Opposite page, bottom: Helicopter tours take you to remote spots, some high up in the mountains.

HIGHLIGHTS FOR KIDS & TEENS:

- Explore the wilderness on playful nature missions, discovering animal tracks and native plants
- Horseback riding, canyoning, and guided adventure hikes
- Boat trips for spotting whales, seals, and sea otters
- Storytelling around the firepit beneath a bright starry sky

ACTIVITIES OFFERED AT THE LODGE:

- Horseback rides and hikes through pristine wilderness
- Canyoning through mountain streams and waterfalls
- Icy plunges in crystal-clear alpine lakes
- Cozy evenings around the firepit

An adventure for the whole family—canyoning on crystal-clear mountain streams.

A spirit of adventure and outpost charm meet stylish living design and modern comfort is how one could describe the 25 tents lining the shores of Clayoquot Sound on Vancouver Island. To reach this luxurious lodge camp set deep in Canada's untamed wilderness, you fly in by seaplane, then travel by horse-drawn carriage through the forest to your tented suite—feeling almost like you are traveling back in time!

The light-filled glamping tents are set on raised veranda platforms, offering views of the water or the lush green forest. Inside, they are simple and cozy, with a refined minimalism that offers comforts such as heated bathroom floors. While luxury touches are present, the real focus here is on experiencing nature and freedom. The lodge follows principles of sustainability, waste reduction, and recycling, and it is dedicated to protecting the wild salmon in the sound.

EXPERIENCE NATURE IN ALL ITS WILD BEAUTY

Every activity here revolves around nature. Head out by boat to spot whales, seals, and sea otters. Go canyoning in crystal-clear mountain streams, climb over rocks, jump into natural pools, and slide down waterfalls. Saddle up for horseback rides through storybook forests or take an icy plunge in hidden alpine lakes. Set off on a mountain bike or paddle a kayak across the sound. For a bird's-eye view, take on a helicopter tour along the spectacularly rugged coastline, landing on remote beaches to explore caves carved by the ocean. Back at the lodge, a dinner awaits, authentic and deliciously made from local ingredients. End the evening by gathering around the firepit to relive the day's adventures.

Top left: Wellness retreat at the spa by the water.

Top right: The horses at Clayoquot Wilderness Lodge are gentle and child-friendly.

Right: A picnic with cocktails high above the clouds.

WHY WE LOVE IT—OUR FAMILY EXPERIENCE:

Our stay at Clayoquot Wilderness Lodge felt like a journey back in time to the Wild West from the very first moment. We were met in true pioneer style by horse-drawn carriage and spent our nights in tents deep in the rainforest, surrounded by pure, untamed nature. Every activity seemed to call out, "Adventure, here we come!" While canyoning, we plunged into icy water, slid through waterfalls, and felt that exhilarating combination of thrill and pride when we made it through. And what would the Canadian Wild West be without a horseback ride through breathtaking forests? Our boat trips to watch seals and whales were equally unforgettable, moments of almost inconceivable natural beauty that will stay with us for a long time. Each evening ended just as an outpost evening should. We were gathered around the firepit, tired but happy, sharing stories of the day's adventures and smiling when the two Clayoquot dogs came trotting by for a visit—wonderful companions who are just as much a part of our memories as everything else at the lodge.

Mountains and Bears

THE NAME SAYS IT ALL: IN BRITISH COLUMBIA'S GREAT BEAR RAINFOREST, YOU CAN EXPERIENCE GRIZZLIES AND BLACK BEARS UP CLOSE LIKE NOWHERE ELSE, WHILE LIVING IN STYLISH LOG CABINS IN THE HEART OF THE WILDERNESS.

Where: In the Great Bear Rainforest in Canada's westernmost province of British Columbia, in the northern foothills of the Pacific Ranges

What: 12 cozy wooden chalets clustered around a pleasant riverside clearing
Vibe: Rustic, cozy, and close to the elements

Tweedsmuir Park Lodge lies where Canada could hardly be any wilder, on the edge of the Great Bear Rainforest, at the foot of British Columbia's Coast Mountains. Amid mighty cedars, crystal-clear rivers, and snow-capped peaks, a clearing along the Atnarko River near Bella Coola reveals one of the best places in the world to see grizzly bears in the wild. Part of the Magnificent 7, a group of Canada's most exclusive wilderness lodges, Tweedsmuir Park Lodge has just a dozen chalets brimming with rustic charm: heavy leather sofas, open fireplaces, and warm wood throughout. The chalets are nestled at the forest's edge with views across a wide meadow, a favorite feeding ground for bears. From the riverside viewing deck, you can quietly and safely watch these majestic animals fishing in the clear waters. The main lodge, with its restaurant, bar, and cozy fireside lounge, embodies classic Canadian charm—the perfect place to share a drink and plan the next day's adventures by the fire following a dinner of locally sourced dishes.

NATURE, BOTH GENTLE AND WILD

Life at Tweedsmuir Park Lodge revolves around the outdoors, from leisurely pursuits to heart-pounding thrills: watching bears just outside your door, rafting on nearby rivers, testing your limits on via ferratas, or discovering the forest in the company of an expert guide. Many excursions start right at the lodge, led by renowned wildlife experts and seasoned guides. As a respectful guest on Nuxalk and Ulkatcho First Nations territory, Tweedsmuir Park Lodge offers its guests the chance to learn about the culture, cuisine, and customs of the Indigenous people during nature walks through the Bella Coola Valley.

HIGHLIGHTS FOR KIDS & TEENS:

- Exciting grizzly bear tours, where safety and respect for nature always come first
- Climbing on the lodge's own via ferrata with professional guidance
- Learning from experts: nature and wildlife education
- Drift boat tours along the river
- Plenty of space for kids to play and roam freely on the expansive grounds

ACTIVITIES OFFERED AT THE RESORT:

- Grizzly and black bear watching tours
- Guided nature walks with ecology experts
- Fishing and rafting
- Helicopter flights over the Bella Coola region
- Experience the culture of the Indigenous First Nations

Left: Children as young as six can take part in via ferrata adventures right at the lodge.

Above: From the viewing platform, you can watch the wildlife along the river and even see grizzly bears right by the camp.

Above left: Those arriving in Bella Coola by plane are treated to breathtaking views of the mountain panorama.

Above right: Along the banks of the Atnarko River, you will find unmatched opportunities to observe grizzly bears in the wild.

WHY WE LOVE IT—OUR FAMILY EXPERIENCE:

The rugged beauty of the Canadian Coast Mountains captivated us from the very first moment we arrived at Tweedsmuir Park Lodge—as did the sheer variety of outdoor activities. We hiked through moss-covered forests, marveled at towering trees, and drifted down the Atnarko River in rafts, always following the tracks of the mighty grizzly bears. We were accompanied by a renowned bear researcher whose deep knowledge and passion for these animals impressed us greatly. One very personal highlight was the via ferrata just a 10-minute drive from the lodge. We faced and conquered our fear of heights, encouraging one another, and were greatly rewarded in the end with sweeping, absolutely breathtaking views across the vast wilderness. Our action-packed days gave way to equally cozy evenings around the crackling campfire. Wrapped in blankets and surrounded by profound silence, we felt nothing but gratitude for the intense, nature-filled family experience Tweedsmuir Park Lodge had given us.

Above: A dozen chalets are clustered around the clearing at Tweedsmuir Park Lodge on the Atnarko River.

Right: Guests gather for meals or a drink by the fire in the lounge at the main lodge.

NIMMO BAY WILDERNESS RESORT

Wilderness by the Water

WHERE ADVENTURE MEETS MINDFULNESS: NIMMO BAY PAIRS THE SERENITY OF WESTERN CANADA'S FJORDS WITH BREATHTAKING EXPERIENCES, FROM HELICOPTER TOURS AND WILDLIFE ENCOUNTERS TO UNFORGETTABLE MOMENTS IN THE REALM OF WHALES AND GRIZZLIES.

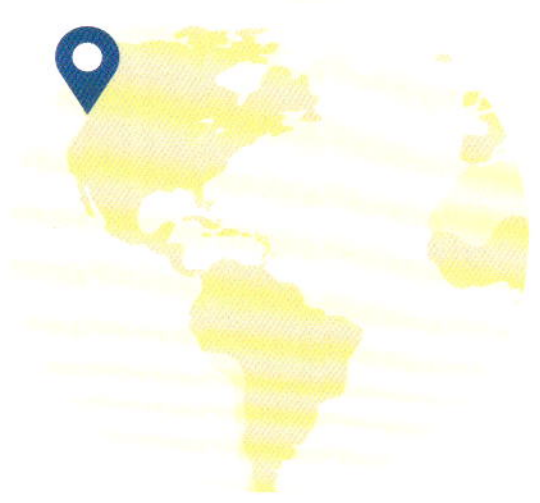

Where: On Mackenzie Sound in Canada's westernmost province, British Columbia, not far from Vancouver Island

What: 9 spacious wooden chalets on the fjord
Vibe: Exclusive, sustainable, and comfortably luxurious

Not far from Queen Charlotte Strait, between Vancouver Island and Canada's Pacific Coast, Nimmo Bay offers the opportunity to experience nature intensively while enjoying all the comforts you desire. This pristine wilderness is the perfect place to reconnect with the natural world. Guests stay in one of just nine cozy chalets nestled among the trees or on the shore of the bay. Each has two bedrooms and, like the rest of the lodge, was built with as little impact as possible on the surrounding ecosystem. The main buildings, including the restaurant, lounges, and a floating fire dock, sit directly on the water, set within the magnificent panorama of the bay.

ABSOLUTE SECLUSION

Nimmo Bay is accessible only by seaplane or boat, and that is precisely what makes it so special. Everything here is far from ordinary. Tailor-made experiences reflect the needs of each guest, regardless of age. The lodge's signature helicopter adventures lead to glaciers, hidden lakes, and picnic spots beside waterfalls accessible only by air. Between kayaking through grizzly territory, whale watching in the fjord, and relaxing in a hot tub under a starry sky, guests find their own balance of adventure and slow living. For children, a day of nature exploration includes exciting activities around the lodge: treasure hunts along the beach, discovering forest secrets, crafting with natural materials, and roasting marshmallows around the campfire. It feels just like a script for their own personal adventure movie.

The comfortably furnished chalets are perched on the shore or nestled in the lush green forest.

Previous page: Wellness on the water in the floating sauna and sun deck.

Below left: Guests can explore the waters of Nimmo Bay on stand-up paddleboards.

Bottom left: Snorkeling reveals a fascinating underwater world.

Below right: Helicopter tours make the beauty of even the most remote places accessible.

HIGHLIGHTS FOR KIDS & TEENS:

- Discovery tours with animal tracking, botanical highlights, and campfire storytelling
- Helicopter flights for little (and big) adventurers
- Kayaking, stand-up paddleboarding, and mini nature missions right by the lodge
- Sustainability workshops offer fascinating insights into the wilderness ecosystem

ACTIVITIES OFFERED AT THE RESORT:

- Helicopter into adventure: hiking, fishing, and picnics in spectacular settings
- Keep an eye out for grizzly bears on kayak trips
- Yoga by a waterfall and spa treatments surrounded by nature
- Private dining on platforms, aboard boats, or deep in the forest

WHY WE LOVE IT—OUR FAMILY EXPERIENCE:

Nimmo Bay gifted us with so many unforgettable moments: We landed on a glacier by helicopter. While the ice crunched beneath our feet, we enjoyed a thoughtfully prepared picnic, followed by drinks at sunset by a remote waterfall accessible only from the air, complete with blankets, drinks, and a fantastic view. Humpback whales and orcas accompanied us on our boat tour in the fjord. And as we paddled our kayaks through a peaceful valley, a young grizzly appeared; we followed him quietly and at a safe distance for a while—a moment of pure, awe-filled serenity.

A List of New Dreams

Andrea Stadlhuber and her team at The Family Project turn vacation dreams into reality for families who want to explore the world with their children. Having personally traveled to many corners of the earth, Andrea is never without one thing: her own personal bucket list.

"I haven't been everywhere, but it's on my list," author Susan Sontag is often quoted as saying, and my family and I feel much the same way. For us, traveling means discovering the most beautiful corners of the world together and giving our children the chance to experience the wonders of nature with their own eyes. I truly believe that every family should have a bucket list, a collection of special places to explore together. It is this wish list of travel dreams, this collection of places we long to see, that fuels our everyday lives and fills us with that special thrill of discovery each time we visit a new place.

Some places you only visit once, carrying them with you as precious memories worth preserving, so beautiful you wish you could capture them in a bottle to keep forever. Other places leave such a deep impression that you return again and again. You want to immerse yourself anew in that special world, hoping they are stil as magical as we remember. And then there are those places that seem to transform with every return, always offering something new to marvel at ...

We hope the destinations featured in this book will provide inspiration for your own personal bucket list. It is impossible to include every single place that has touched us on our travels, but we would still like to share a few that are close to our hearts. In South Africa, we were enchanted by Ulusaba, with its mesmerizing views, and Singita Lebombo, with its distinctive design. On Likoma Island in Malawi, the colorful, bohemian-style Kaya Mawa unfolds its own magic along the lakeshore. In the Arab world, the spectacular location of Six Senses Zighy Bay in Oman, the majestic Qasr Al Sarab Desert Resort in Abu Dhabi, and the traditional Kasbah Tamadot in Morocco's Atlas Mountains left us in awe. On Bali's Uluwatu cliffs, the Bulgari Resort treated us to world-class cuisine, while Soneva Kiri on the Thai island of Koh Kood delighted us with its playful Robinson Crusoe vibe. In Malaysia, The Datai Langkawi is a true icon of tropical elegance, and in the United States, nestled in the endless expanse of Utah, Amangiri remains etched in our memory as a retreat of profound strength and clarity.

And then there are the places we still dream of—destinations that have long held a special place atop our family bucket list; places we hope to soon explore. One of these is the extraordinary Nay Palad in the Philippines, the epitome of barefoot luxury, freedom, and effortlessness. As you turn the pages ahead, we invite you to browse our personal wish list and join us on a journey to the places that continue to capture our hearts and imagination.

COMO LAUCALA

A South Seas Idyll at World's End

WHITE BEACHES, THE LUSH GREEN RAINFOREST, COCONUT PLANTATIONS ON MOUNTAIN SLOPES, AND THE TURQUOISE BLUE LAGOON ALL AROUND YOU: THE PRIVATE ISLAND RESORT OF COMO LAUCALA IS EVERYTHING YOU COULD POSSIBLY IMAGINE WHEN DREAMING OF THE SOUTH SEAS …

Where: On a private island in the north of the Fiji Islands, near the third largest island of Taveuni

What: 25 spacious villas with pools and gardens

Vibe: Completely private, exclusive, and in the heart of nature

Left: Horseback riding on the beach is an experience for horse lovers of all ages.

Opposite page, top: Tropical palm trees on a romantic walk along the beach (left) and surrounding the luxurious villas (right).

Opposite page, bottom: Absolutely breathtaking—a glass infinity pool floats at the center of the expansive pool landscape.

Below: The transition from the pool area to the sandy beach and on to the ocean is seamless.

Opposite page, top: Cocktails with spectacular architecture as a backdrop—the beach bar by the pool lagoon is a true eye-catcher.

Opposite page, bottom: The 18-hole golf course, framed by palm trees and the ocean, is simply idyllic!

HIGHLIGHTS FOR KIDS & TEENS:

- In-house childcare with creative discovery programs
- Fun in the water in sheltered lagoons: swimming, snorkeling, and paddling
- Experiences with animals, plants, and crafts on the farm
- Island adventure activities: horseback riding, fishing, beachside adventures, and small boat trips

ACTIVITIES OFFERED AT THE RESORT:

- Snorkeling, fishing, diving, sailing, kite surfing, wakeboarding, and Fliteboards
- Horseback riding, mountain biking, hiking, picnics, and exploring the island
- Tennis courts and a golf course with spectacular ocean views
- Wellness, stretching sessions, farm tours, and cooking classes
- Individual boat excursions

Como Laucala is a resort beyond compare—existing in another dimension altogether, it redefines privacy, quality, and the experience of nature in sustainable harmony. Covering almost 3,500 acres, this private island in the north of Fiji is twice the size of Manhattan, yet home to just 25 opulently furnished villas scattered along the ocean, nestled in the jungle, or perched on mountain ridges. The traditional Fijian architecture combines natural materials with elegant interior design and the highest level of comfort. True to the South Seas, indoor and outdoor spaces flow seamlessly into one another, fully immersing guests in the island's breathtaking surroundings. And there is no shortage of things to discover and experience: horseback riding along the beach, diving on the reef, water sports and snorkeling in the crystalline lagoon, hiking and mountain biking through the rainforest, and playing tennis and golf on a spectacular 18-hole course. A children's club with a friendly childcare staff offers a wide variety of activities. Culinary pleasures are equally abundant, from surprise picnics in secluded spots to local and international delicacies served in the island's three restaurants. Many of the ingredients come from Laucala's own organic farm or the surrounding ocean—fresher, more flavorful, and more authentic than you could imagine.

WHY WE WANT TO GO—A PERSONAL NOTE:

We long to discover the magic of the South Seas: the dazzling colors, the wonderful soft light, the atmosphere of serenity and tranquility that seems to infuse everything. These put Como Laucala at the very top of our wish list, and not even the long journey to Fiji will deter us. What draws us most is the nature: so lush, unspoiled, and vibrant. The vastness, the naturalness, the space to breathe—it all comes together here in a very special way. And so we are certain that one day soon our South Seas dream will come true on this island paradise ...

KISAWA SANCTUARY

Wildness and Wellness

AN ISLAND OF WHITE BEACHES MELTING INTO TURQUOISE WATERS, WITH WILD DUNES AND AN ABUNDANT, DIVERSE VEGETATION BEHIND THEM—AT ITS HEART, CURATED RESIDENCES OFFER EVERY LUXURY WHILE BLENDING SEAMLESSLY WITH NATURE. KISAWA REDEFINES THE EXCLUSIVE BEACH ESCAPE.

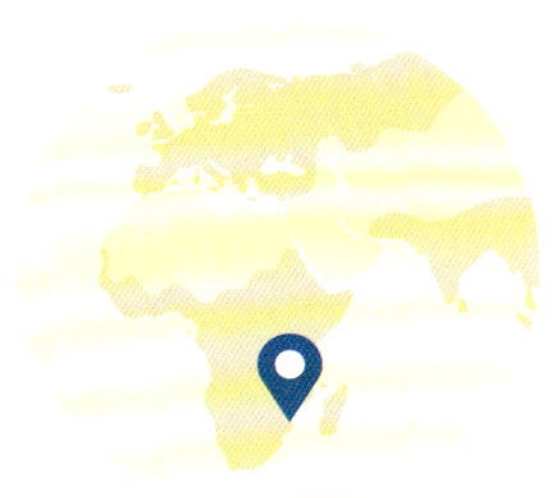

Where: Private nature reserve on Benguerra Island in the Bazaruto Archipelago off the coast of Mozambique

What: 8 spacious villas, each with its own infinity pool and terrace
Vibe: Elegant, right in the heart of nature

Combining luxury and exclusivity with the preservation of flora and fauna, while fostering an awareness of local culture and life—this is Kisawa Sanctuary's mission. Spanning almost 750 acres, the private nature reserve feels like paradise. Just eight villas lie tucked into the dunes and along the broad sandy beach. Each is spacious, elegantly furnished, and equipped with every comfort, from a private infinity pool on the vast terrace to dedicated butler service. Every villa also comes with its own electric Mini Moke, allowing guests to explore the sweeping dune landscape at their leisure. The rhythm of the tides, the brilliance of the ocean, the warmth of the island's people—Kisawa brings it all together in harmony, naturally and understated, creating experiences that are all the more profound.

Guests can take a boat out to watch whales and flamingos, join marine biologists at work, explore the lagoon by kayak, stand-up paddleboard, or sailboat, soar through the air while kite-surfing, or go snorkeling and immerse themselves in the underwater world. Between adventures, there is always time to be pampered in the serene spa retreat or simply take in the island's natural beauty.

WHY WE WANT TO GO—A PERSONAL NOTE:

Kisawa is the next beach resort on our list—and we can hardly wait! Everything we have read and seen so far sounds irresistible, and just a glimpse of the villas is enough to get us dreaming: open to the landscape, thoughtfully designed, stylish, and in perfect harmony with their surroundings. On a previous trip, we already fell in love with the magnificent nature of Benguerra Island. We adore its pristine beaches, its dunes, and the fascinating interplay of high and low tides across the vast coastal landscape—as well as the natural simplicity that makes the island so special. And then there are the warm, welcoming, and open-hearted people we truly look forward to seeing.

Above: Nowhere are the dynamics of high and low tide more impressively displayed than in the vast lagoon seascape off Benguerra Island.

Right: Nestled among palm trees, dunes, and the ocean, the villas offer the utmost privacy.

Relax in the spa with yoga and Ayurvedic treatments in harmony with nature.

Enjoy a drink at sunset in the outdoor lounge before discovering Mediterranean or Mozambican cuisine in one of the restaurants.

Elegant and spacious—the bathrooms in the residences look like private spas.

HIGHLIGHTS FOR KIDS & TEENS:

- Swimming and snorkeling in the calm waters in front of the villa
- Learning about local conservation projects on nature walks and in workshops
- Whale-watching boat trips and an excursion to Flamingo Beach
- Experiencing life in the island villages, playing soccer with schoolchildren
- Overnight camping in the dunes under the starry skies
- Making pizza on the beach

ACTIVITIES OFFERED AT THE RESORT:

- Snorkeling on the house reef
- Sunset cocktails on the dunes, boat tours, and picnics
- Spa retreats, meditation, and beach yoga
- Exploring the island by electric Mini Moke
- Visiting the on-site marine research center
- Experiencing local culture and daily life through encounters with the community

Dinner on the beach in a magical natural setting.

MIAVANA

Luxury, Lightness, and Lemurs

OFF THE COAST OF MADAGASCAR, HOME TO CAPTIVATING LEMURS AND MAJESTIC, CENTURIES-OLD BAOBAB TREES, MIAVANA OFFERS A UNIQUE COMBINATION OF ULTIMATE BAREFOOT LUXURY AND PRISTINE NATURE.

Opposite page: Miavana Piazza, with its restaurant, lounge, and vast pool area, sits directly on the beach, nestled among palm trees.

Above: From the stylish bar and lounge, the view opens onto the endless ocean—the perfect spot for sunset drinks.

Right: Here you can encounter playful lemurs—found only in Madagascar and on Miavana's private offshore island.

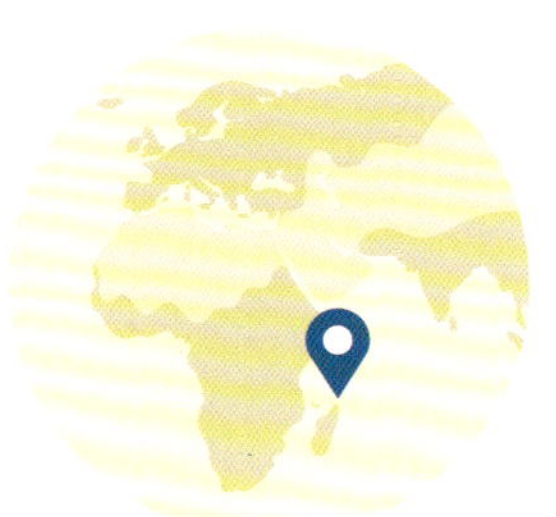

Where: On the private island of Nosy Ankao off the northeastern coast of Madagascar in the Indian Ocean

What: 14 villas with one to three residential units, each with a private pool and terrace
Vibe: Barefoot luxury—free, relaxed, and close to nature

Miavana's spacious villas, furnished with warm materials, are situated directly on the beach.

Off the Malagasy coast, on the private island of Nosy Ankao, lies one of the Indian Ocean's best-kept secrets: Miavana, Madagascar's unique retreat and a spectacular gateway to a fascinating natural paradise. Just 14 spacious beachfront villas make up this exclusive resort, each offering all the barefoot luxury one could wish for: a private pool, personal butler service, your own beach buggy, and above all, complete privacy. Yet despite all its comfort, Miavana never loses sight of the island's raw, untamed spirit, the very essence that makes this extraordinary corner of the world so unique. In the midst of a 37,000-acre marine reserve, surrounded by the vast ocean and snow-white beaches, unforgettable adventures await on land, on and in the water, and even in the air. Track down lemurs, explore the island by buggy, marvel at the iconic baobab trees of the nearby mainland on a scenic helicopter flight, dive and snorkel on the reef, glide across turquoise waters by kayak or on a stand-up paddleboard, and feel the thrill and freedom of kitesurfing. For quieter moments, the spa offers relaxation. Children, too, are treated to tailor-made experiences, always with a focus on the island's ecosystem and its conservation under the resort's care.

WHY WE WANT TO GO—A PERSONAL NOTE:

Madagascar has always fascinated us. This island is different, a land of contrasts, bursting with life. Our journey to Miavana, this dreamlike island resort, has long been planned, but as life would have it, it has remained only a dream so far. Still, we keep imagining the legendary Avenue of the Baobabs in the light of the setting sun, the playful lemurs, the wind dancing through the dunes, and the ever-changing patterns the sea creates with each tide. From everything we have read, Miavana weaves itself effortlessly into this picture: a resort deeply in tune with nature, finely balancing authenticity, comfort, and adventure. We cannot wait to finally experience it for ourselves.

HIGHLIGHTS FOR KIDS & TEENS:

- Snorkeling, fishing, kayaking, and discovering turtles
- Hunting for shells and fossils
- Nature hikes and night safaris to spot lemurs on the mainland
- Learning about biodiversity, constellations, and conservation

ACTIVITIES OFFERED AT THE RESORT:

- Helicopter flights to the Tsingy rock formations or baobab forests
- Diving, kitesurfing, stand-up paddleboarding, deep-sea fishing tours
- Sunset boat rides and picnics on deserted islands
- Relax at the spa, stargazing, and with gin and tonics by the campfire

Clockwise from above: Miavana offers a variety of exclusive activities, from diving on the reef to sunset fly fishing and kitesurfing in the turquoise waters.

SONEVA SECRET

A Secret Paradise on the Sea

HIDDEN AWAY IN A SECLUDED MALDIVIAN ATOLL, SONEVA SECRET BLENDS THE FINESSE OF MODERN LUXURY WITH A DEEP CONNECTION TO NATURE THROUGH ITS ECO-CONSCIOUS DESIGN, CREATING TAILORED, ONE-OF-A-KIND EXPERIENCES.

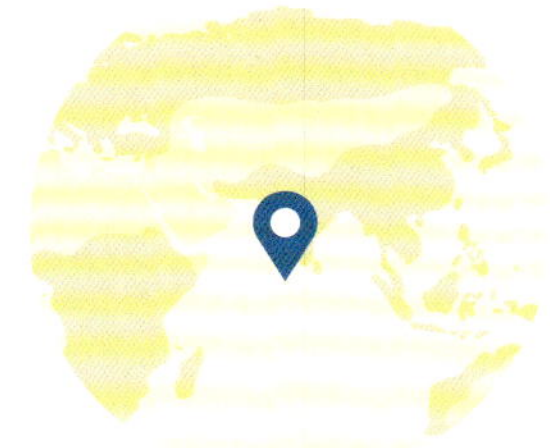

Where: On a private island in Makunudhoo Atoll in the north of the Maldives

What: 14 luxurious villas with private pools
Vibe: The most exclusive barefoot luxury, absolutely private and in tune with nature

Soneva Secret creates space for truly immersive experiences, precisely because this private island lies far from everything except the extraordinary aquatic world surrounding it. Its 14 villas—some over the water, some on the beach, and one entirely secluded in the lagoon—embody everything that defines the Soneva philosophy: an elegant ambiance, private pools (some with the iconic waterslides), and retractable roofs that let you gaze at the stars right from your bed. Exclusive service reaches a new level here, as each villa not only comes with a private butler but also with a dedicated chef, allowing guests to enjoy every comfort without ever leaving their luxurious hideaway. Of course, there are plenty of reasons to venture outside: three restaurants—one reached by a spectacular zipline arrival, an observatory where the island astronomer shares the wonders of the night sky, an open-air movie theater on the beach, and countless activities ranging from night snorkeling with manta rays and diving on the reef to nature-inspired workshops and spa visits. The children's club is as versatile, creative, and attentively managed as in other Soneva resorts.

WHY WE WANT TO GO—A PERSONAL NOTE:

We love the Maldives—and places where nature, architecture, and sustainable philosophy come together in perfect harmony like they do at Soneva. That is why Soneva Secret, the newest and perhaps most exclusive of all Soneva's dream hideaways, tops our wish list. Everything we love about barefoot luxury is taken one step further here: the ultimate privacy of the stunning overwater villas and the unmatched turquoise of the pristine lagoon, paired with a level of personalized service that promises pure perfection.

Previous pages: In the exclusive villas poised above the turquoise lagoon, guests can enjoy sweeping views across the endless ocean.

Opposite page: The beachfront villas also promise exquisite luxury in a completely private oasis.

Below left: This private island in Makunudhoo Atoll offers total seclusion—the ultimate Robinson Crusoe experience. Sliding from your villa straight into the ocean never gets old.

Below right: At the observatory, the resident astronomer interprets the wonders of the star-filled night sky.

HIGHLIGHTS FOR KIDS & TEENS:

- Reef snorkeling and ocean watching right outside your villa
- Making pizza with your private chef
- Nature discovery, treasure hunts, and creative workshops
- Open-air movies over the water
- Outdoor planetarium with child-friendly stargazing sessions

ACTIVITIES OFFERED AT THE RESORT:

- Snorkeling and diving in pristine coral reefs
- Private dining experiences on sandbanks or in the jungle
- Spa treatments, yoga, and meditation
- Sustainable experiences: reef clean-ups, visits to the island's horticultural nursery, and marine biology insights

PICTURE CREDITS

Cover: © Nihi Sumba

Back cover: top left: © Velaa Private Island, top right: © Andrea Stadlhuber, bottom left: © Andrea Stadlhuber, bottom right: © Nihi Sumba

p. 5: © Andrea Stadlhuber
p. 7: © Time & Tide Chongwe Lodge
p. 8: © Islas Secas
pp. 10-11: © Schloss Elmau
p. 12 top: © Andrea Stadlhuber
p. 12 bottom: © Frégate Island
pp. 13-14: © Frégate Island
p. 16: © Andrea Stadlhuber
p. 17 top: © Andrea Stadlhuber
p. 17 bottom: © Frégate Island
pp. 18-20: © Andrea Stadlhuber
p. 21: © North Island
p. 23 left: © Six Senses Zil Pasyon
p. 23 right: © Andrea Stadlhuber
p. 24 top left and bottom: © Six Senses Zil Pasyon
p. 24 top right: © Andrea Stadlhuber
p. 25: © Six Senses Zil Pasyon
p. 27 top left: © Soneva Fushi
p. 27 bottom left and right: © Andrea Stadlhuber
pp. 28-29: © Soneva Fushi
p. 30: © Soneva Jani
p. 31 top: © Soneva Jani
p. 31 bottom: © Andrea Stadlhuber
p. 32: © Soneva Jani
p. 33: © Andrea Stadlhuber
pp. 34/35: © The Nautilus Maldives
p. 36: © Andrea Stadlhuber
p. 37: © The Nautilus Maldives
p. 39 left: © Andrea Stadlhuber
p. 39 top right and bottom: © Como Maalifushi
pp. 40-41: © Como Maalifushi
p. 42-43: © Patina
p. 44: © Andrea Stadlhuber
p. 45 top left and right: © Andrea Stadlhuber
p. 45 bottom: © Patina
pp. 46/47: © Velaa Private Island
p. 48: © Velaa Private Island
p. 49 top left: © Velaa Private Island
p. 49 bottom left: © Andrea Stadlhuber
p. 49 right: © Velaa Private Island
pp. 50/51: © Ceylon Tea Trails
p. 52 left: © Andrea Stadlhuber
p. 52 right: © Ceylon Tea Trails
p. 53: © Andrea Stadlhuber
p. 55 top left: © Wild Coast Tented
p. 55 bottom left: © Andrea Stadlhuber
p. 55 top right and bottom: © Wild Coast Tented
pp. 57-58: © Cape Weligama
p. 59 left: © Cape Weligama
p. 59 right: © Andrea Stadlhuber
pp. 60-64: © Nihi Sumba
p. 65: © Andrea Stadlhuber
pp. 66/67: © Bawah Reserve
p. 68: © Bawah Reserve
p. 69: © Andrea Stadlhuber
p. 70: © Capella Ubud
p. 71 top left: © Andrea Stadlhuber
p. 71 top right and bottom: © Capella Ubud
p. 72: © Andrea Stadlhuber
p. 73: © Capella Ubud
pp. 74/75: © Four Seasons Resort Koh Samui
p. 76: © Four Seasons Resort Koh Samui
p. 77 top left and bottom: © Four Seasons Resort Koh Samui
p. 77 right: © Andrea Stadlhuber
p. 78: © Song Saa
p. 80: © Song Saa
p. 81 left: © Andrea Stadlhuber
p. 81 right: © Song Saa
p. 82: © Andrea Stadlhuber
p. 83: © Zannier Phum Baitang
p. 84: © Andrea Stadlhuber
p. 85: © Zannier Phum Baitang
pp. 86-87: © Six Senses Ninh Van Bay
p. 88 left: © Andrea Stadlhuber
p. 88 right: © Six Senses Ninh Van Bay
p. 89: © Six Senses Ninh Van Bay
p. 91 left and top right: © Six Senses Con Dao
p. 91 bottom right: © Andres Stadlhuber
pp. 92-93: © Six Senses Con Dao
pp. 94-95: © Liz Biden
p. 97 left top: © Royal Malewane
p. 97 bottom left and right: © Andrea Stadlhuber
pp. 98-99: © Royal Malewane
p. 101: © La Residence
p. 102 top left and bottom: © La Residence
p. 102 right: © Andrea Stadlhuber
p. 103: © La Residence
p. 104: © The Silo
p. 105: © Andrea Stadlhuber
p. 106: © The Silo
p. 107 left: © Andrea Stadlhuber
p. 107 right: © The Silo
p. 108: © Tswalu Kalahari Reserve
p. 109 top left: © Andrea Stadlhuber
p. 109 top right and bottom: © Tswalu Kalahari Reserve
p. 110: © Andrea Stadlhuber
p. 111: © Tswalu Kalahari Reserve
p. 112: © Marataba
p. 113 top: © Marataba
p. 113 bottom: © Andrea Stadlhuber
p. 114: © Andrea Stadlhuber
p. 115 left: © Marataba
p. 115 right: © Andrea Stadlhuber
p. 117 left: © Babylonstoren
p. 117 top right and bottom: © Andrea Stadlhuber
pp. 118-119: © Babylonstoren
p. 120: © Grootbos
p. 121 top: © Grootbos
p. 121 bottom: © Andrea Stadlhuber
p. 122: © Grootbos
p. 123 left: © Grootbos
p. 123 right: © Andrea Stadlhuber
p. 124/125: © Sonop
p. 126: © Sonop
p. 127: © Andrea Stadlhuber
p. 128: © andBeyond Sossusvlei Desert Lodge
pp. 129-130: © Andrea Stadlhuber
p. 131: © andBeyond Sossusvlei Desert Lodge
p. 132: © Wilderness Serra Cafema
p. 133: © Andrea Stadlhuber
pp. 134-135: © Wilderness Serra Cafema
pp. 136-137: © San Camp
p. 138: © Andrea Stadlhuber
p. 139: © Jack's Camp
p. 141 left: © Andrea Stadlhuber
p. 141 right: © Wilderness Jao Camp
p. 142 top left and bottom: © Wilderness Jao Camp
p. 142 top right: © Andrea Stadlhuber
p. 143: © Wilderness Jao Camp
pp. 144/145: © Wilderness Duma Tau
p. 146: © Wilderness Duma Tau
p. 147 left: © Wilderness Duma Tau
p. 147 right: © Andrea Stadlhuber
pp. 148-149: © Matetsi Victoria Falls
p. 150: © Andrea Stadlhuber
p. 151 top: © Matetsi Victoria Falls
p. 151 bottom: © Andrea Stadlhuber
pp. 152/153: © Time & Tide Chongwe
p. 154: © Time & Tide Chongwe
p. 155 left: © Andrea Stadlhuber
p. 155 right: © Time & Tide Chongwe
p. 157 top left and right: © Time & Tide Chinzombo
p. 157 bottom left and right: © Andrea Stadlhuber
pp. 158-159: © Segera
p. 161: © Andrea Stadlhuber
pp. 162-163: © Segera
pp. 164/165: © Giraffe Manor
p. 166: © Giraffe Manor
p. 167 left: © Andrea Stadlhuber
p. 167 right: © Giraffe Manor
p. 169 top left and bottom: © Solio Lodge
p. 169 right: © Andrea Stadlhuber
pp. 170-171: © Solio Lodge
p. 172: © Andrea Stadlhuber
p. 173 top left: © Andrea Stadlhuber
p. 173 top right and bottom: © Legendary Expeditions – Mwiba Lodge
p. 174: © Andrea Stadlhuber
p. 175: © Legendary Expeditions – Mwiba Lodge
p. 176: © Chem Chem Safari Lodge
p. 177 top: © Chem Chem Safari Lodge
p. 177 bottom: © Andrea Stadlhuber
p. 178: © Chem Chem Safari Lodge
p. 179: © Andrea Stadlhuber
p. 180: © andBeyond Mnemba Island
p.181: © Andrea Stadlhuber
pp. 182-183: © andBeyond Mnemba Island
pp. 184-185: © Borgo Egnazia
p. 186: © Borgo Egnazia
p. 187 top: © Borgo Egnazia
p. 187 bottom: © Andrea Stadlhuber
p. 188: © Borgo Egnazia
p. 189 left: © Andrea Stadlhuber
p. 189 right: © Borgo Egnazia
p. 191 left: © Domaine de Murtoli
p. 191 right: © Andrea Stadlhuber
p. 192: © Andrea Stadlhuber
p. 193: © Domaine de Murtoli
p. 194/195: © Porto Zante
p. 196: © Porto Zante
p. 197 left: © Porto Zante
p. 197 right: © Andrea Stadlhuber
pp. 198-199: © Amanzoe
p. 200 left: © Amanzoe
p. 200 right: © Andrea Stadlhuber
p. 201: © Amanzoe
pp. 202-205: © Schloss Elmau
pp. 206-208: © Bachmair Weissach
p. 209 left: © Andrea Stadlhuber

p. 209 right: © Bachmair Weissach
p. 210: © Andrea Stadlhuber
p. 211: © Benjamin Zibner
p. 212: © Andrea Stadlhuber
p. 213: © Tom Kohler
p. 215: © Andrea Stadlhuber
pp. 216-217: © Sublime Comporta
pp. 218-220: © Ashford Castle
p. 221: © Andrea Stadlhuber
p. 223: © Katrin Kirchhoff
p. 225 left: © Morgan's Rock
p. 225 right: © Andrea Stadlhuber
p. 226: © Morgan's Rock
p. 227 top left: © Andrea Stadlhuber
p. 227 top right and bottom: © Morgan's Rock
p. 228: © Origins Luxury Lodges
p. 229 top: © Origins Luxury Lodges
p. 229 bottom: © Andrea Stadlhuber
p. 230: © Origins Luxury Lodges
p. 231 left: © Origins Luxury Lodges
p. 231 right: © Andrea Stadlhuber
pp. 232/233: © Nayara Tented Camp
p. 234: © Nayara Tented Camp
p. 235: © Andrea Stadlhuber
p. 237 left: © Islas Secas
p. 237 top right: © Andrea Stadlhuber
p. 237 bottom right: © Islas Secas
p. 238 top: © Andrea Stadlhuber
p. 238 bottom: © Islas Secas
p. 239 top: © Andrea Stadlhuber
p. 239 bottom: © Islas Secas
pp. 240-241: © Clayoquot Wilderness Lodge
p. 242: © Andrea Stadlhuber
p. 243 top left and bottom: © Clayoquot Wilderness Lodge
p. 243 top right: © Andrea Stadlhuber
p. 245 left: © Andrea Stadlhuber
p. 245 right: © Tweedsmuir Park Lodge
p. 246 left: © Andrea Stadlhuber
p. 246 right: © Tweedsmuir Park Lodge
p. 247: © Tweedsmuir Park Lodge
pp. 248/249: © Jeremy Koreski
p. 250: © Jeremy Koreski
p. 251 top left and bottom: © Jeremy Koreski
p. 252 right: © Andrea Stadlhuber
p. 253 top left: @ Kisawa Sanctuary
p. 253 top right: © Miavana
p. 253 bottom left: © Soneva Secret
p. 253 bottom right: © Como Laucala
pp. 254-257: © Como Laucala
pp. 259-261: © Kisawa Sanctuary
pp. 262-265: © Miavana
pp. 266/267: © Soneva Secret
pp. 268-269: © Soneva Secret

World maps: Designed by Freepik

ABOUT THE AUTHOR

"Traveling with children adds depth to every journey—it reveals what a precious gift it is to share unique experiences with your loved ones." Guided by this belief, travel expert Andrea Stadlhuber, born in Munich in 1977 and mother of three, founded her company The Family Project in 2016. After earning a degree in business administration at the LMU in Munich and working in marketing, she combined her professional experience with her passion for discovering the world's most beautiful places.

Today, she inspires families who treasure extraordinary experiences to embark on adventurous journeys across the globe, from the idyllic islands of the Indian Ocean to Africa's wild terrains and hidden paradises in Asia. Together with her experienced team, who individually tailor each itinerary, she demonstrates how the wishes of children and the preferences of adults can blend harmoniously.

Andrea Stadlhuber understands the needs of discerning families. For over two decades, she has traveled the world with her husband and sons, exploring its most fascinating destinations. "I want to show families that adventure doesn't end when you have children."

With *Family Escapes*, she shares a handpicked collection of exceptional destinations, curated from a decade of intensive travel as a family of five.

ACKNOWLEDGEMENTS

This book is my personal expression of gratitude to all those who, with courage, vision, and dedication, have created extraordinary places that touch our hearts, filling us with so much joy time and again.

For Maxi, Ali, and Consti—the best travel companions I could ever wish for—and for my husband, Matthias, who blindly puts his trust in me when it comes to planning our journeys and is always open to new adventures.

With my deepest appreciation, I thank our exceptional interview partners and icons of the hospitality world who graciously shared their stories for this book.

My sincere thanks also go to all those who supported me so wonderfully in bringing this project to life, from layout to photography and copy: to Luisa Krause-Rossa for ensuring seamless coordination, to Eva Stadler for her beautiful design and inspired selection of pictures, and to Anja Klaffenbach for professionally and perceptively refining my writing.

From the bottom of my heart, I thank my colleague Katrin Sepmeier (Head of Portfolio Management, The Family Project) for her tireless communication with our partner hotels, and last but not least, my colleague Sandra Wimmer (Head of Sales, The Family Project), whose 30 years of experience in the luxury travel industry, together with our wonderful team, makes these and other dream destinations possible for our clients and their families.

Andrea Stadlhuber

Edited by Andrea Stadlhuber,
The Family Project GmbH & Co. KG
Texts by Anja Klaffenbach

Translation by Robin Limmeroth

Editorial Management: Luisa Krause-Rossa, gestalten
Design and Layout: Eva Stadler
Production: Nele Jansen, gestalten
Image Editing: Nele Funck and Robert Kuhlendahl, gestalten

Printed in Germany by aprinta druck GmbH

Produced in Europe

Published by gestalten, Berlin 2025
ISBN 978-3-96171-725-5

1st printing, 2025

The german edition is available under
ISBN 978-3-96171-728-6.

For more information and to order books, please visit www.teneues.com and www.gestalten.com

Die Gestalten Verlag GmbH & Co. KG
Mariannenstraße 9–10
10999 Berlin, Germany
hello@gestalten.com

Düsseldorf Office
Waldenburger Straße 13
41564 Kaarst, Germany
verlag@teneues.com

teNeues Press Department
press@gestalten.com

Bibliographic information published by the Deutsche Nationalbibliothek. The Deutsche Nationalbibliothek lists this publication in the Deutsche Nationalbibliografie; detailed bibliographic data is available online at www.dnb.de

instagram.com/teneuespublishing

www.teneues.com

The Family Project GmbH & Co. KG,
Thann 17, 84544 Aschau am Inn,
hello@the-family-project.com

instagram.com/the_family_project

www.the-family-project.com